EDNA'S
TABLE

EDNA'S
TABLE

JENNICE AND RAYMOND KERSH

Hodder & Stoughton

Everything happened at Edna's Table

We ate at Edna's Table

We laughed at Edna's Table

My father often pounded Edna's Table

Raymond sewed on Edna's Table

Tommy, our baby sister, was adored and cherished at Edna's Table

Mum iced her magnificent cakes at her table

People confessed at Edna's Table

Abe prepared great food on Edna's Table

Babies' nappies were lovingly changed by Edna at her table

People sought condolence from Edna at her table

All children were quietly listened to at Edna's table

Abe yelled frequently at Edna's Table

People were reassured by Edna at her table

Raymond constantly created beautiful works of art at Edna's Table

People were given hope at Edna's Table

Tommy relished defying Abe at Edna's Table

Edna gave her meals away at Edna's Table

We constantly debated at Edna's Table

Edna's manners were of the best at her table

Edna quietly shared everything she had at her table

Relations and friends sang from their Boomerang song books at Edna's Table.

Mum and dad encouraged our discussions around Edna's Table

Jennice and John arrogantly thought they taught Edna at her table

Dad danced on Edna's Table

Raymond always observed wisely at Edna's Table

First Sean then all her grandchildren were glorified by Edna at her table

Being Jewish, Dad welcomed his new son-in-law, Doctor Fraser at Edna's Table

Edna's children tried to shock her at Edna's Table

Abe drank too much at Edna's Table

Mum embraced Gavin as her son at Edna's Table

Mum made scones and tea for Munja at Edna's Table

Abe swore often at Edna's Table

All races were part of the extended family at Edna's Table

In Kent Street Raymond created a new Edna's Table

Mum and dad loved this Edna's Table

All of those in our lives followed us to mum's new table

Bianca and Rowan performed frequently at Edna's Table

Alex and James and many children followed them at Edna's Table

Rowan, like a giant cockroach, was chased by staff at Edna's Table

We said goodbye to Mum and Dad at Edna's Table

Christmas eve 1989 our hearts were broken when we had to close Edna's Table.

October 1993, proud for what is Australian, we opened our new Edna's Table

Christmas 1997 a new generation of children had inherited all that is Edna's Table

Warm friendships have been forged at this Edna's Table

We now realise how much we learnt at Edna's Table

May mum's splendid spirit live on at Edna's Table

EDNA'S
TABLE

A Hodder & Stoughton Book

First published in 1998
by Hodder Headline Australia Pty Limited
(A member of the Hodder Headline Group)
10-16 South Street, Rydalmere NSW 2116

Published in association with
Brewster Publishers
P.O. Box 3231, Tamarama NSW 2026

National Library of Australia Cataloguing-in-Publication data
Kersh, Jennice.
    Edna's Table.

    Includes index.
    ISBN 0 7336 0539 7.
    1. Cookery, Australian. I.Kersh, Raymond. II. Edna's Table
    (Restaurant). III. Title.

641.5994

Printed in Hong Kong

Produced by Phoenix Offset

ACKNOWLEDGEMENTS

We would like to thank the following people:

Our brother John, who was responsible for our love affair with the Australian outback and our introduction to the beautiful Gogadjas, the indigenous people of Balgo Hills in the Kimberleys.

Rolf Petherbridge and Graham Fear, who believed in and supported the embryo of our endeavour, helped make its birth possible and sustained its growth.

Dearest Min Keating, whose confidence in our commitment to native produce is reminiscent of Edna's.

Michael and Kerry Carlton, whose friendship and advice have grown through turbulent times.

Judith White, our kindred soul, who thought that readers would find our story, and in particular the account of our humble but proud beginnings, worthy of print.

Pam Seaborn, who stands proud as an Australian and who recognised our dreamtime and ultimate embrace of this unique country—a determined and priceless friend.

Christine Seaegg, our mutual lifelong friend, who shared our journey to Balgo and our love of food, who understands our frailties and has always been there.

Kimberley Kersh, who as a builder worked tirelessly with us to create Edna's Table II and who truly shares our vision for these indigenous foods.

Ray's precious son Strath, who has patiently observed in the wings, with the wisdom of a sage, the demands of this profession and of this book.

Mundara and Yvonne Koorang, our urban Aboriginal artist friends, whose generosity is an inspiration.

David Koch (Kochie), whose encouragement for our interpretation of native produce has never wavered.

Pat Dasey, for not just listening but truly understanding who we are.

Pam Brewster, a fine and sensitive lady, whose patience was challenged and won, who against the odds believed in our message and Lisa Highton, who allowed us, through Hodder, to tell our story.

Oliver and Ernie, whose photography has given the one-time embryo of this book a wonderful and believable body.

Margaret Fulton, the grande dame of Australian cooking, who insisted we write the book but wisely warned us how all-consuming it would be.

The writers without whose sheer energy most people would never have heard or read of the existence of native Australian produce, let alone the indigenous cuisine of Edna's Table II, and whose individual efforts are greatly appreciated: Lindey Milan, Peter Howard, John Newton, Diane Holuigue, David Dale, Sheridan Rogers, Mardi Kerr, Graham Kerr and Bruce Kraig.

The kitchen team at Edna's Table, who laboured long writing Raymond's recipes.

The floor staff, who kept the home fires burning while Jennice worked on the script.

David Jones, Wedgewood and Lifestyle Imports for providing the beautiful plates used throughout the book.

Gabriella Roy of Aboriginal & Pacific Art for allowing us to use their artworks.

Last but certainly not least the small but valiant band, to which Raymond and I are so proud to belong, of pioneers of Australian native ingredients, in particular Vik Cherikoff, Jean-Paul Bruneteau, Andrew Fielke and Alan East.

CONT

ENTS

FOREWORD

Even the great cooks have their recipe disasters, and Raymond's was the Chocolate Chicken. God knows how or where he came by it, and when I first saw it on the menu at the old Edna's Table a few years ago I assumed it was some sort of practical joke.

But it wasn't. It was chicken done in chocolate—or perhaps chocolate done in chicken, I can be no more certain than that—and it was, according to his sister, Jennice, a famous Mexican delicacy. She wasn't too sure about it herself, but Ray had decided to give it a whirl to see what would happen.

The answer is that not much happened. You got chook and you got chockie, all stuck together, and it was awful: the Easter bunny meets KFC. I think I was the only customer who tried it, and very reluctantly. With a notable absence of Mexicans beating a path to Edna's door to feast on this inventive example of their national cuisine, the dish quietly vanished from the menu within a week, never to be seen again.

But the story says a lot about Ray Kersh. He is an artist of the kitchen who is never afraid to take risks, a creative chef always eager to experiment with his art, to push the boundaries out a little further. Like the man on the flying trapeze he may have fallen once or twice in the learning process, but the performance has been a triumph.

The first Edna's Table was in Kent Street in downtown Sydney, only a few blocks from the radio station where I was working in the mad, bad old '80s, and I stumbled

MIKE CARLTON

across it pretty much by accident when Jennice bought some advertising time in my program. Within about a week, I think, it became the station's office canteen. We were always going there, always there, or always just about to leave.

The place was a bit crazy because the times were a bit crazy. As the great Sydney boom just kept on booming, lunch became a long day's journey into night, and not only for idle journalists and radio people but for a rainbow cross-section of the city's life. Judges and jockeys, politicians and punters, sopranos and stockbrokers, doctors and developers, company directors and cabbies flocked to be there—partly for the food, partly for the fun.

And fun it was. The kitchen stood smack bang in the centre of the room, with Ray and his crew chopping and slicing and grilling and frying in full view of the tables. It was like watching sorcerers at work, or perhaps conjurers. Every so often a sheet of flame would shoot towards the ceiling as some cognac hit a hot sauté pan and then, magically, your perfect meal would smoothly appear from what looked like utter chaos.

Jennice seemed to know everyone, and everyone knew Jennice. If Ray was the master of the stove, she was the mistress of the tables. Her welcome was friendly and gay—genuinely gay in the old sense of the word—with a complete absence of either the fake servility or the haughty 'We're doing you a favour just letting you in the door' attitude you strike in too many big city restaurants. Everyone was met with the same grace and courtesy, whether arriving for the first time or the two hundredth.

I think this spontaneous warmth sprang from their childhood in the knockabout waterfront suburb of Pyrmont. Abe Kersh was a waterside worker, 'Australia's only Jewish wharfie,' as Jennice always said. Edna, whose name lives on, was one of those motherly Catholic ladies whose door was always open and whose stove was always hot. And if times were tough occasionally, they were never too hard to spread a feast on Edna's table for a neighbourhood celebration.

So when it came to running a restaurant, the Kershs, you knew, were genuinely pleased to see you. Which meant that people were genuinely pleased to be there. Jennice would always have the latest joke or the latest news, and the regulars grew to know each other, would wave to each other, would table hop for drinks before and after. Conversation sparkled, friendships were forged, and some traditions began to blossom.

Or explode, which might be a better word. There are three truly remarkable and eagerly awaited seasons in the Edna's calendar: St Patrick's Day, Melbourne Cup Day, and the weeks before Christmas. Guests book months in advance—some have a more or less permanent reservation—and the room is packed to the rafters, ringing with hilarity and good cheer and the singing of Irish ballads, not so much a restaurant as a theatrical performance. Aboriginal musicians mix with opera singers, Irish folk dancers with classical string quartets. Heaven help us, on Pat's Day we actually had a blind potato tasting, adjudicated by a distinguished if more than slightly hazy member of the judiciary.

But behind all the frolic and the frivolity, the Kershs had a serious purpose. More than that: they had a dream. Some adventurous spirit, a wanderlust, called them away from the wharves and the tight little streets of terraces where they grew up and led them to discover the vast,

although never empty, spaces of the Australian continent.

From the noise and hustle of the big smoke they travelled north and west, and gradually they came to know and then to admire and to love the indigenous people of this land. And it was there, among the Aboriginal tribes, that the Kersh dream began to take shape and form. Ray and Jennice, artists both, had discovered a new canvas to paint with fresh and brilliant colour. It would be a genuinely Australian canvas.

For the 200 years since white settlement, Australian food has had its origins overseas. In the beginning, it was mostly British with a dash of Irish: roast and three veg stews and stodgy puddings. Then, with the great wave of immigration after the Second World War, we embraced Mediterranean cuisines and styles of Asian cooking, our tastes becoming more experimental and more varied with each generation.

But it has been only in the past few years, perhaps ten at most, that a handful of chefs slowly have come to realise what the Koori people have known for centuries: that a wealth of flavours and ingredients lie waiting for us, native to our own country. Ray Kersh was at the forefront of those early white pioneers. He still is.

The closing of the first Edna's after a battle with a landlord seemed like a disaster at the time. It was a hard blow to the brother and sister and a grievous disappointment to their legions of friends and fans. But with hindsight it was a blessing, for as one door closed, another opened.

That new door was the inspirational Edna's Table II, in Sydney's MLC Centre in the heart of the city between King Street and Martin Place. Against all the advice of their friends, me included—it'll never work, you'll go broke in a month, etc.—the Kershs set their hearts on opening a stylish restaurant with an Aboriginal theme to the decor and with food that would reflect the variety and abundance of Australian ingredients they had discovered in their travels.

I am not sure what some of us expected; perhaps a few boomerangs and didgeridoos nailed to the walls, and there were lots of jokes about wombats and witchetty grubs. But we should have known better. Ray and Jennice called upon the help of their Aboriginal spirit to create a room that is itself a work of art, with its warm ochre colours, the bold painted grass trees curving up the walls, and stark white sculptures. Raymond supervised every detail with infinite patience and precision, down to the design of the chairs.

And then there was the food: crocodile and kangaroo, yabbies and oysters, buffalo and bunya nuts, warrigul greens and wattleseed, bush tomatoes, wild limes and mountain pepperleaf, Davidson plums. Over long days and nights of blending and tasting, rejecting and accepting, the Kershs gradually but surely evolved a new and unique Australian cuisine which combined classical techniques with the rich array of native textures and flavours they had discovered. The dream had become reality.

Which is what this book is about. It is the story of their remarkable journey to bridge a cultural divide, to span the chasm between European and Aboriginal existence. At the risk of sounding madly pretentious, that journey is a metaphor for Australia itself as our country feels its way towards the reconciliation of white and black that will painfully but inevitably happen in the next century.

That said, this is also a good, plain, do-it-yourself cookbook. Those native foods and ingredients which Ray and Jennice once found so difficult to obtain are now becoming an everyday sight on the shelves of delicatessens and supermarkets around the nation as suppliers meet the growing demand. Call it bush tucker if you want to, call it Australian cuisine if you will, but this book will be the instruction manual for cooks everywhere who want to follow in Ray Kersh's trailblazing footsteps.

Or, if that's too hard, there's always the welcome awaiting you at the restaurant. No more Chocolate Chicken, but book early for St Patrick's Day.

COOKING UP
AUSTRALIA

If a fortune teller had told me thirty years ago that I'd become a chef and run a well-known restaurant with my younger sister Jennice, I would have thought they were crazy. But that's exactly what happened and this book is the story of that journey, and of our passion for the wonderful native food and ingredients that are found throughout Australia.

In Australia in the 1970s, the top restaurants were mostly French. The menu was written in French and the food was cooked in the French style. I remember going to a swish restaurant and ordering something I thought would be really special. When it came out, it was just roast chicken and peas, dressed in brown sauce! Even that long ago I knew there had to be good food you could offer people that wasn't pseudo-French.

When we opened the first Edna's Table in the early 1980s we wanted to say we were Australian. In those days you couldn't get native foods, but a wider variety of produce was becoming available—things like kiwi fruit, macadamia nuts and tamarillos. I tried to push the possibilities of what was available.

Food writers found it hard to label us and used to call us French, which riled me. There was no French on the menu or in the menu. Australians had a great cultural cringe, so with Edna's Table I suppose I was out to prove a point—not just that we can develop our own style, but that we can use the ingredients that grow here naturally.

When I started to cook I had only been to a couple of

RAYMOND KERSH

dozen restaurants because if you were working class you really had to save up to do it. When I did go I was always a bit disappointed that people didn't make an effort—you walked out not feeling special. It had cost you a lot and you didn't enjoy the experience. I'd say to Jennice, 'Gee, we could have bought Mum half a fridge for that!' So I wasn't as big on restaurants as Jennice was. I'd always thought they were a bit of a rip-off. It's ironic that I ended up running them—but I never forgot my initial feelings.

I'm happy to share my recipes in this book because I know home cooks in Australia are often quite prepared to have a go at reproducing interesting new flavours. We grew up with a love of food because my dad, Abe Kersh,

was the best home cook of all time.

I didn't begin as a chef. I was a couturier who made high fashion clothes for a living. I'd just finished making all the costumes for the Music Hall, a leading Sydney theatre at the time, and the Australian Ballet had asked me to join their costume department as part of the team for the next season's productions. This was a great honour and I was looking forward to the challenge. But it wasn't to be. Jennice had taken my younger sister Margaret to Terrigal to convalesce after a spinal operation. I was the eldest in the family and a sort of surrogate dad for my sisters. They needed me there with them, so without much enthusiasm I left the city and headed north. Though I wasn't aware of it at the time, that journey changed my life profoundly: it was in Terrigal that I took the first timid steps towards becoming a professional chef and restaurateur.

As there wasn't much call for high fashion in Terrigal in those days, I took a temporary job in the kitchen of the Hotel Florida where Jennice was working—a very glamorous, upmarket hotel. On the very first night there was a rush and the second chef was having trouble keeping up with the orders, so I made some sweets just to help him out. The head chef, an American called Woody, took one look at the way they were presented, tasted one, and offered me a job on the spot as his breakfast and barbecue chef. As I had no credentials and there was a strict hierarchy in kitchens, this was a great compliment.

One thing I found bizarre at the Florida was that orders were supposed to be called out in French in the kitchen. It seemed very out of place, particularly in the mouth of the sous-chef, Roger, who was covered in tattoos, wore earrings before it was fashionable for men to do so, and rode a Harley Davidson everywhere—even through both storeys of The Pines, the weatherboard guesthouse where most of the staff stayed. Straining to hear Roger struggling with his French pronunciation through his ill-fitting false teeth was something you just didn't need in the middle of the lunch rush.

Looking back now, I think the fact that I didn't have a classic training made me the kind of chef I am. I have always felt a free spirit in the kitchen. Because I didn't know the rules, I broke them all (and still do!). Finding the new ingredient, the new sauce, the new combination that produces a true marriage of flavours eventually turned into a passion. As I became more experienced as a chef, I became more adventurous and found the outlet for creativity I had always got designing clothes.

Buffets were all the rage in those days, and the Florida used to do big Hawaiian-style luaus, where the centrepiece on the table was a roast pig with an apple in its mouth. I thought we could offer something more imaginative, so I turned the pig into a sculpture. I piled fruits high on its head like Carmen Miranda and sculpted a skirt from scalloped ornamental cabbage, lettuce and other vegetable leaves.

However, my road to Damascus with regard to food wasn't the Hotel Florida's big barbecue. It was Kim's Camp, a nearby resort at Toowoon Bay. The owner was an eccentric English colonel and he opened up a whole new world for me. He cared passionately about every aspect of food—its quality, its preparation, its presentation. He went to great lengths to provide variety and balance in the menus, and handed down to those who worked there an invaluable repertoire of dishes from the great cuisines of other countries. It was a real learning curve. I came to understand there was a world of difference between just cooking food to eat and creating a cuisine. A chef is like a painter or a composer or an architect. They can be just as creative and can reach a very high plane of perfection. That's why people often refer to a dish as 'sublime'—it evokes the same kind of intense response in people as does a beautiful piece of music.

The colonel came from an aristocratic family. His brother was Admiral of the Fleet in London—or so he said. He was 'teddibly, teddibly' English and had lived in India under the Raj. He was a gourmet and owned a large collection of recipe books and food magazines, which he read like novels. He'd pick out the things he liked for the menu and include Indian dishes he knew which were entirely different from anything we recognised as a curry in Australia at that time. He'd carefully explain what should happen in the recipe, then he'd watch over it as it was prepared, tasting and adjusting. He was very much the owner of all the dishes we served.

Kim's Camp taught me two important things: that there was more to food than just cooking, and that I was good at cooking. I was enjoying it more and more and wanted to change recipes to give them 'my' touch. I was never scared of using exotic ingredients because of my father,

who always cooked us very unusual meals—what everybody else called 'foreign' dishes. He just melted into what he was creating and there was nothing we kids were scared of in food. So I had an adventurous side that I had inherited from Dad.

Jennice and I then went to Dunk Island to upgrade the restaurant and facilities of the resort. I was to work with Martin, a German chef who had been trained in the classic European tradition. Technique was his middle name and he taught me all his skills. Like all good Germans, Martin loved sweets and made superb desserts and cakes. Wandering around the tropical gardens and the surrounding national park, I discovered wonderful things growing wild—native wild lime, lemon myrtle, and other fruits and berries. By this time I was cooking my own dishes, and I would use these ingredients in tarts and puddings and main courses. When I first made a tart out of the wild limes, Martin looked horrified and said, 'But you can't use them. We don't know what they are. They might be poisonous!' I told him I'd been eating them for weeks and I was still alive. And they were delicious. That tart became a favourite with guests all the time I was there. I used lemon myrtle a lot, too. Martin was a very fine chef and I learned essential lessons from him, but there was a great difference in our approach to food. His was conservative, mine was experimental and innovative—and remains so to this day.

One of the biggest influences on the style and food of Edna's Table was my visit to the Great Sandy Desert and the magnificent Kimberley Mountains in Western Australia. I was bowled over by the grandeur of the landscape and the great mountains. When I saw the Kimberleys I understood the meaning of the word 'spiritual'. It was a combination of magnificent colours and shapes, the sense of space and the awareness of our place in the universe. It was frightening, too. An artist friend told us years later he was so spooked one night camping in the desert that he packed up and came home.

Later the Aborigines said he was 'in the wrong place at the wrong time' and told him there were many spirits there. You are very much aware of spirits in the desert. You get a much greater understanding of why the land is so important to Aborigines.

Jennice and I had gone to visit my brother, John, who had set up a program to breed cattle and stock horses and train Aboriginal stockmen at Balgo Hills Mission Station. When visitors today ask me 'What's Australia like?', in my head I immediately think of the Kimberleys. But I don't tell them that because I know they'll never get there and wouldn't understand. Most Australians have no idea of what the bulk of this country really looks like.

At Balgo I tasted some of the native foods, but I didn't know what half of them were and later, when I was cooking more seriously, they weren't available commercially. However, the sounds, the sights, the tastes, the wildlife, the beauty—all my positive impressions of the Kimberleys—were stored in my subconscious and surfaced many years later in 1987 when we were asked to make a submission for a restaurant in Darling Harbour. I could see the ceilings painted with Aboriginal designs, the spinifex grass I was going to have in a kind of fibreglass, the didgeridoo player, the desert colours. There would be symbols representing the four elements of earth, fire, air and water. But above all, it was going to be an Australian restaurant. I even made up a menu that had emu, kangaroo and crocodile dishes on it, and those meats were illegal for general consumption in New South Wales at the time. All this was a very unusual concept in those days, and it didn't come to fruition. But I kept the dream, and when we came to open the present Edna's Table it came true. Those Australian dishes that didn't exist in restaurants then—emu, kangaroo, crocodile—are now our most popular requests.

I was always proud of Australian things, even when I

ASPARAGUS TEMPURA WITH BEAN QUONDONG ORANGE CHILLI SALAD PG **68**

was a young dressmaker. But my fantasies of an Australian fashion industry didn't get anywhere in the 1950s. Despite Dad and his European background and the many nationalities that we met at our house, I always felt like an Australian kid with a very working-class Aussie background. And proud of it.

At the first Edna's Table restaurant I became more adventurous with food, combining ingredients in unexpected ways: rhubarb with mint, asparagus with pink peppercorns, fish with macadamia nuts and mustard seed sauce, for example. We served buffalo, rabbit, venison and goat, even stuffed sheep's hearts—which was a disaster, because although it tasted delicious most people are very conventional about food and were scared to try it.

The present Edna's Table is everything Jennice and I wanted in a restaurant—a place where people feel at home and hopefully go away feeling they've had a really special night. By the time we opened there was a regular supply of twelve Australian ingredients available, and you could legally serve meats such as emu and kangaroo. When you compare our very first menu in 1993 with our current one, you can see how Australian food tastes have matured and how I was able to develop challenging dishes as more ingredients became available. For instance, though we did have char-grilled kangaroo fillet, I had to liven up traditional favourites such as roasted chicken or rack of lamb by using unusual ingredients—native aniseed, wild rosella buds, warrigal greens. I was deliberately more adventurous with entrees: using an Illawarra plum salsa with char-grilled octopus, curing salmon with lemon myrtle (a heavenly combination) and stuffing miniature 'swag bags' with yabbies and serving them with a bush tomato sauce. The most daring things were an emu and native mint ravioli and gumleaf-smoked wild buffalo carpaccio served with roasted red capsicum, warrigal greens and Tasmanian pepperberry salad.

STIR-FRIED SCAMPI, MUNTHARI BERRIES AND ASIAN GREENS PG **89**

Australians have become more adventurous eaters and are always looking for new things. We've been influenced enormously by Japanese and Thai food and have long embraced Italian, so I've used the best techniques of Asian and European countries and applied the same principles to Australian native food; for instance, we now serve a roasted rare emu fillet, with pear wrapped in crispy pancetta and a munthari berry and balsamic vinaigrette. This demands a highly developed palate and a sophistication to appreciate the subtle combination of flavours. I could never have served this three years ago. This recipe came to me when I saw a bottle of apple balsamic vinegar and a light went on in my brain. If you can make vinegar with apples, you might be able to use pears with a vinaigrette. I developed this dish with my talented young chef, Matt Peade.

Today it's very satisfying to see our clients responding to the challenge of innovative food. And I'm not just talking about the raw produce (emu, crocodile, kangaroo), but the complexity of the dish as a whole. We now bake fish in paperbark, make pestos out of native ingredients, wrap food in seaweed and rice paper, deep fry tempuras but serve them with delicious native Australian sauces. We use Australian herbs and berries to make pasta, aioli, hollandaise, chutneys, even sabayon (a wonderful combination is fresh asparagus with Botany Bay greens and a lemon and native thyme sabayon). I adapt native ingredients and use them in the traditional styles we've come to love from other countries to develop a true Australian cuisine. It's not modern Australian, it's eternally Australian. And as far as I can see it's just the beginning of an exciting gastronomy we can offer the rest of the world.

Except for the emphasis on Australian native food, our restaurant is still the place it always was, and looking after the customers is still as important as the food. The spirit of my parents, Edna and Abe, is still there—I think they would have liked this place.

FOOD FROM OUR LAND

This book isn't just about food. It is about our identity—not just Raymond's and mine, but the identity we all share as Australians. From the moment Raymond and I opened the second Edna's Table in 1993, this was the conception. Australian native ingredients were now available commercially, so there were a lot of dishes we wanted to do that we could now source. To us it was natural to create a look that went with the food, and that meant going back to the amazing time we spent in the desert. It left a spiritual imprint in both of us that only grows with time. So when Raymond decided that he would create the shapes and colours and flavours of his country, both in the interior of the restaurant and on the menu, we were very excited.

We believed that Australians would start to look at what we have in this country and use what grows here naturally, instead of always trying to grow what comes from another land. Having a brother on the land, we were influenced by the struggle of farmers with the drought—an often unnecessary struggle, it seemed to us. European Australians haven't always looked at our country sufficiently to see the enormous array of foods, of timber, of natural resources that can grow in a land with not a great deal of topsoil. We continually plant things here from countries where the soil is so much richer.

The land produces them, of course. We're often surprised by how much it yields. We always have big celebrations on special days, and some years ago we held

JENNICE KERSH

the inaugural Edna's Table Guinness Stout World Potato Tasting Championship as part of our St Patrick's Day events. In the course of it we found out that Australia produces twenty-eight different types of potato. It was, by the way, one of the most hilarious things we've ever done. People had to guess what variety of potato they were tasting. The prize was four dozen bottles of Guinness and a bottle of Jameson Irish Whiskey. The prize was so popular that cheating became rife, especially among the judges. Lindey Milan, the food writer, was beside herself at the extent of the foul play.

But we thought later that if this country can produce such variety in an imported vegetable, the scope for developing native foods is enormous.

We had been developing dishes with native produce for quite some time before it dawned on us that we were among just a handful of people doing so, and that it wasn't the most normal thing in the world for many people. For a while that was dispiriting. But when there is a passion for anything, that is the strongest force. Without it there's no pioneering spirit. So we just kept on pursuing what we were doing. We have never tried to be different in our lives. We just done what we believed in.

When we opened Edna's Table II we found that a lot of Australians were hesitant about what we were doing. But it's fascinating how you can seduce people with food. Thai food has become enormously popular in this country in the past fifteen years—people taste it when they travel to

Thailand, they see ingredients like coriander in the markets, they have the cookbooks. There's a familiarity. With what we're using, a lot of people have never even seen the ingredients. So right from the beginning, creating our menu was all about seduction—having dishes on the menu that people love, like roast lamb rump, but slipping in something different like an Illawarra plum salsa with rocket. Soon people began to eat the food and like it almost without noticing.

I know as well as anyone that using unknown, exotic ingredients involves all kinds of difficulties. Once we had a group of European scientists in the restaurant. As I was telling them about the day's menu one of the guests, a charming and sexy Italian professor, asked about the salad of rare gumleaf-smoked emu fillet and quandong (wild peach). 'What is emu?' he asked. I explained that it is a native bird similar in appearance to the ostrich. He looked round at the rest of the table and fixed me with an inquiring smile. 'But,' he said, 'why does it have a condom?'

Australians have embraced a rich variety of European and Asian cuisines in the thirty-three years Raymond and I have been working in the restaurant business. We firmly believe that they will now begin to turn to the food of our land. No home cook should be afraid to try my brother's recipes. After all, our love affair with food began around my mother Edna's table in a tiny two-bedroom council flat in Pyrmont, eating the amazing meals created by our father, Abe.

Everything important in our lives happened at Edna's table. Relatives and friends poured out their troubles. Babies' nappies were lovingly changed. We sang songs from our Boomerang song books. My brother Raymond would often be sewing down one end while Edna decorated one of her famous cakes at the other. An endless stream of friends and relatives were comforted, encouraged and loved. Mum's hospitality and Dad's

magnificent food embraced our little Pyrmont community and made up for the hardship of growing up in grinding poverty.

Years later, when we were looking for a name for our first restaurant, Raymond said he wanted it to be a tribute to Mum's spirit and warmth, and to the meals we'd enjoyed around her table. The name just seemed to stick. Edna was the centre of our family. She had a wicked sense of humour and could laugh at herself better than anybody in the world. She was self-effacing, unpretentious and hated snobbery in any form. She found people endlessly fascinating and they were drawn to her lovely, warm personality like a magnet.

Abe Kersh was a crusty, hard-drinking man, a gambler, bright and eccentric, with an incredible talent for food. He worked as a wharf labourer on the docks and in Pyrmont, the working-class, Irish Catholic suburb that had grown up around a busy passenger and cargo wharf on Sydney Harbour. Everything my father ate, he cooked. He didn't ever ask how to cook it and he never owned a recipe book. No matter what it was, he could make a replica of it. And if he didn't have an ingredient, he would just improvise with something else that would make it equally stunning. Food wasn't just a hobby, it was an all-consuming part of his life.

Our flat was on the top floor of a large Mediterranean-style council block. It had a million-dollar view of the harbour, and every day we'd sit on our verandah watching the sun set over the church steeples of Balmain. It was a tight-knit little village where everyone knew everyone. They gossiped about each other, fought with each other and cared for each other in the bad times. There was Fred the gardener, Spiro the Greek milk bar proprietor, Basil who owned the Chinese fish and chip shop, Chris the postman, Barney the barber, Mr Conlon the baker, Mrs Dempsey, the assertive publican at The Terminus, the most revered Mr Watk, who taught everyone to swim, Alf the fruit man, Mr and Mrs Shelly and Mr McGrath from

Maybank Council Playground, and Mrs Ferg (short for Ferguson), who owned the general store. They were all very much part of our community life. Lily Ferg, who was a tall and forthright woman, saved many a family from starvation through her kindness. Wharfies in those days were paid a pittance and treated badly by the ship owners. Mrs Ferg let their wives, if they were low on money, put the groceries 'on the bill' until they could pay. She never once refused a person credit, no matter what the circumstances. Looking back, it's a wonder she made any money at all.

That was the spirit of Pyrmont and I loved it. It is deep in my soul, and my elder brothers, Raymond and John, and my younger sister, Margaret, all have the same intense feeling about growing up there. It was so full of life, so colourful and chaotic. The overseas terminal was there then and, in those days, most people travelled abroad by ship. Many of the people who disembarked were migrants starting a new life here, but most were sophisticated and beautifully dressed. They ate the finest food on board, prepared by top chefs. When the ships sailed, two bands played, and we kids would wrap ourselves in the thick curtains of multicoloured streamers that smothered the boat, the passengers and those waving goodbye.

There were Chinese, Italian, Greek, Swedish, French, Russian and British ships with the sounds of foreign languages ringing out all day long. Indian Muslims, their prayer aprons tied around their waists, paid homage to Allah in the street—it didn't matter where they happened to be—several times a day. Cranes unloaded cargo and trucks carted goods away. Crossing the road could be life-threatening for kids, and my uncle was incapacitated for life when he had his leg crushed by a wool bale falling on top of him.

The first thing Dad did when a ship came in was to introduce himself to the chef. He learned to make authentic Indian curries by watching the Indian crews on the British liners cooking their traditional food, squatting over little burners on deck. Ships were often in port for five or six days, so Abe would invite the chefs home for meals. It wasn't hard to guess what we'd be eating then for the next three weeks! I was three when I first ate one of my father's curries, and I cried. Abe thought this was a very good sign. A curry was no good unless it was fiery and brought tears to your eyes. If you didn't cry, you had no palate. I cried buckets, begged for more, and went up several notches in my father's estimation. We became very used to a multicultural diet. Other people's food often seemed bland and boring in comparison.

Till the day he died, Dad also continued to cook every meal his grandmother used to make. She was born in Russia to a strict Orthodox Jewish family. They fled to London during a pogrom and she married there, then came to Sydney soon after. Abe adored his grandmother. She used to sit him on the kitchen bench with her while she prepared meals; she was a wonderful cook. As a consequence, the Kersh kids ate foods that were unheard of in Pyrmont in the 1940s and 1950s: black bread, soused herrings, gefillte fish, smelly cheese. My father and brothers had fish and lobster traps and crab snares down below the wharves. Dad's gefillte fish was different from everybody else's; he'd add chopped parsley or mint, some chopped prawns (he was proudly Jewish, but not religious), then he'd poach the fish cakes, cool them, refry them in a little peanut oil and add the final touch—some soy sauce and fresh ginger. They were heaven.

Abe often got the devil in him, especially after fifteen schooners of beer. Our house was next-door to a field which Dad, for some reason, took to calling 'Mrs Paddock'. If something wasn't to his liking on the night he'd been to the pub, he'd simply pick up the object of his derision and hurl it through the window saying, 'Maybe Mrs Paddock might like this.' My best friend, Billy Dillon, and I used to race downstairs and have a competition to see who could catch what dad had thrown

before it hit the ground. We didn't bother if it was one of Mum's meals. Dad hated Mum's Anglo-Celtic food. 'Edna,' he used to say, 'the Jews crucified Christ but you crucify every meal you ever make!' Mum was a lovely cook—but it was traditional British/Irish food with bland vegetables, and that wasn't what Dad was about at all.

One of the things we loved to eat most was smoked fish roe. In those days it wasn't known in Pyrmont, and we kids used to fight to get it. We'd spread it on crumpets and toast and try to make it last because it was expensive. When Dad caught mullet he used to smoke his own fish roe, which I thought was much better than the bought variety. Uncle Jack across the road was retired and owned a little wooden launch called the 'Old Duck' in which they often went way outside Sydney Heads to go fishing. Uncle Jack had a smoker in his tiny backyard, and when he got a big catch he'd give Dad a lot of the fish. Abe would cook some fresh in some gorgeous way and distribute it to neighbours (and the local barmaid!), then he'd souse and pickle, marinate or smoke the rest. Even people who didn't like fish would eat it if Abe Kersh had cooked it.

Abe also made his own cheese. He used leftover milk that had gone sour, tied the cheese in a cloth and hung it up to cure over the kitchen sink. As it matured it developed a rich and unpleasant odour and, even worse, dripped all over whoever was unfortunate enough to be washing-up below. Ray and John would rush home from school and polish off the milk to make sure none was left for a new batch of cheese. There were sighs of relief in our house when refrigeration finally arrived.

My father was the world's worst gambler, but two or three times a year he would win at the races. On these joyous occasions he would take us all to Chinatown for a meal. Everyone selected a dish and Abe would order another couple. Then he would come home and reproduce them all. You couldn't buy bok choy and other

THE KERSCH FAMILY - TOP: JOHN, EDNA, ABE, RAYMOND
BOTTOM: MARGARET, JENNICE

Chinese vegetables we take for granted today, but Abe would substitute European-style vegetables, add an exotic spice or two and cook them the Chinese way. After he worked on a Japanese ship he was soon cooking 'Abe's sukiyaki'—a stunning stir-fried dish using long julienned strips of meat and vegetables, especially mushrooms which he loved. He often bought vegetables that weren't commonly known from Paddy's Market, which back then was where the Sydney Entertainment Centre stands today. He had a great feel for interpreting such ingredients into a foreign cuisine.

All the visitors to our home in Pyrmont sat in the kitchen because the lounge room was so small and stuffed with furniture that you couldn't move. It became even more crowded when Edna bought the world's biggest pianola. We'd been to see the wonderful black American pianist Winifred Atwell when she visited Australia; Abe was totally enthralled and had visions of his little Jennice becoming a white Winifred. He wanted me to have lessons and ordered Edna to find a piano. The problem was, Mum had no savings. She was a cleaner and Dad loved the horses and his beer, so there was never any spare money. With the help of a friendly credit company, Edna came home with a pianola that would take her at least thirty years to pay off. It was so big it had to be taken apart and hoisted up through the top floor. With it came 200 free piano rolls. From then on the pianola became the second love in Dad's life. He'd be on it until three o'clock in the morning and drive the poor neighbours mad. Initially they loved to hear the tunes, but as his enthusiasm increased they could have cheerfully chopped both him and the pianola to little pieces. Dad's parties now took on a whole new dimension. During the week, half the pub would come home with him when the doors closed to hear the pianola. He would hand around cigars and Edna, ever hospitable, would prepare an impromptu midnight supper at her table. She was always a good sport.

I never did learn to play the piano.

EDNA'S
TABLE

How so many people squeezed around the table in that tiny kitchen I'll never know. Raymond would cut out his patterns on the floor then clear the table to finish off the sewing. Sewing is Ray's version of meditation; he does all his thinking while he's sewing. When we were growing up, if you went to his machine and sewed even a few centimetres he would know. He knew if you'd even breathed on his machine. He's only just replaced the one Mum gave him thirty-five years ago. Raymond sewed for everyone in Pyrmont for nothing. By the time he was twenty-one he would have made 100 bridal frocks and the bridesmaids' dresses, not to mention the clothes he made for Edna, Margaret and me.

One day he'd just finished making this gorgeous bridal frock that had taken days of detailed work. He shook it out to have a look, and, to his horror, there was a great big food splodge down the front because poor Edna hadn't wiped the table properly after dinner. I learned that day that Raymond had inherited Dad's terrible temper. He had also inherited Abe's gift for creating unique dishes, though it wasn't to surface till many years later.

On Sundays the pubs weren't open—officially, that is. Abe and his mates used to join the sly grog crowd in the garden at the back of The Terminus. Today the pub is no longer in use but it still stands, and the door still bears a dent worn by the rat-tat-tat of the sly grog customers tapping on it with a penny. As we kids grew older we soon worked out where Dad was. He would have been up at six o'clock in the morning cooking our traditional Sunday breakfast extravaganza, and he often took selections of exotic morsels he'd prepared so the regulars could try them. He was so vain that he loved it when they all told him how good his cooking was. 'Look at him,' my big brother John would say, 'he only does it for the praise.' But I was delighted my father's food was getting the appreciation it deserved. Maybe I inherited his love of adulation. Billy Dillon, John and I thought we were the bee's knees when we began to sneak into the pub to entertain the drinkers. I suppose I was a bit of an extrovert even then. We were so busy lapping up the applause for our song-and-dance act that it never occurred to us to keep tabs on John. He might be a respectable farmer now, and the loving father of nine well-brought-up children, but it has occurred to me that he did very nicely out of passing the hat round while we were taking bow after bow.

If he wasn't at The Terminus Abe would be cooking. On Sunday our home was always chaotic, full of relatives, friends, neighbours and laughter. Mum's aunt, Aunty Annie, was very fat and jolly and loved to dance. So she would be jiggling around the kitchen playing the mouth organ or gnawing on a lamb shank. Dad would be cooking up a storm, telling terrible jokes or yakking with his wharfie cronies. Ray would be trying to sew, Edna would have the usual horde of children underfoot—and our grandparents and aunts and uncles would be putting in their tuppence worth about everything, in particular about how we should be reared. It was bedlam and we loved every minute of it.

New Year's Eve was a special event on the Kersh calendar. We had a big party every year and Dad did his Al Jolson and Eddie Cantor impersonations (because they were Jewish). We'd cross hands at midnight and sing 'Auld Lang Syne' and Dad, who'd had a few too many, would start to cry. As the tears flowed he'd promise to stop drinking and gambling, to be a better father and husband, and of course Edna believed him. She must have, because John, Margaret and I were all born in October, obviously the result of New Year's Eve euphoria and Dad's good intentions. So every New Year's Eve as midnight chimed, my brothers would groan, 'Oh no, here come the tears again!'

There was always spirited and open discussion in our home. My parents encouraged us to have an opinion in the days when children were supposed to be seen and not heard. Looking back, although there was sadness at times because of Dad's atrocious behaviour when he drank too much, there was a lot of laughter and a great deal of love. Humour was our salvation and got us all through the worst times. I know in my heart that certain things that happened in our home have affected me for the rest of my life, but I am sure we survived through our ability to laugh about any situation. We even laughed about tragedy and in the face of tragedy.

Though we didn't know it, our childhood was very bohemian, and full of larger-than-life characters. They just loved to visit this crazy home and sit at Edna's table, enjoying Abe's wonderful food. Little wonder Ray and I ended up in the restaurant business which is, after all, only an extension of our childhood.

When I was about twelve and Raymond was already apprenticed as a tailor, our family used to visit Canyonleigh, near Moss Vale in the Southern Highlands. An Englishman, Gerry Gadogon, worked at White Bay Power Station where Mum ran the canteen. He became a close friend and was often at our flat. His bachelor brothers Pat and Leo were soldier-settlers and had a 3,000-acre station called The Whip out in the country. Gerry's best mate at the power station had a car, and so did Billy Dillon—one of the very few people in Pyrmont who did. So between the two of them we would often get taken down there for weekends or holidays.

It was here that I first ate the meats of Australia— kangaroo and wallaby, wood ducks, wild pigeons and other wild birds (they used to make a delicious wild duck stew), even snake and eel. Pat and Leo didn't eat these foods just to be exotic and adventurous; they were poor and it was all just food to them. I started to cook here in my own right, not just heating up the meals Mum prepared for us when she was on shift work, and I loved experimenting with the simple spices Pat and Leo had at hand. Eating kangaroo or wild meat never worried me because I was used to Dad's cuisine, and I came to love the flavours.

An experience in my early teens left a lasting impression and influenced me years later as a restaurateur. Raymond used to make suits for two charming Italian gentlemen who owned and ran a restaurant called the Astor, in the famous apartment building in Macquarie Street. Occasionally they invited us to dine with them. I can still remember the wonderful atmosphere: opera music played in the background, the setting was beautiful Art Deco, the service impeccable and the food stunning. I ate homemade ravioli for the first time, unheard of where I grew up. To this day I've never eaten Italian better than that served at the Astor. And the Astor taught me that a restaurant wasn't just about food—it was a total experience. Making people welcome was just as important as the food. When I stop enjoying serving people I'll close the doors, because the pleasure of cooking that we learnt from Dad and the joy of my mother's hospitality are what drive Raymond and me.

In our twenties we took to the restaurant business, working together first in Terrigal at the Hotel Florida and then on Dunk Island. By now our brother, John, a farmer and a lay missionary, was married and living with his wife, Norah, and two small children on Balgo Hills Mission Station, a remote place out in the Kimberleys. He'd gone there to set up an ambitious cattle station and stock horse breeding program, crossing horses with the wild brumbies that roamed the area in great numbers. We decided to visit him. With absolutely no idea of the distance, we thought we'd just go to Cairns and hop across the top. Easy. In the event it took weeks to travel the thousands of kilometres. Balgo Station alone was over two million hectares. John used to visit Wyndham and Alice Springs once a year to pick up non-perishable supplies. As luck would have it, his annual pilgrimage to Wyndham was scheduled three weeks after we arrived, so he drove us back to Balgo. There were 300 people or more on the mission, so John had quite a shopping list.

Wyndham was a wonderful, crazy town. Up in the Top End you get the runaways, the eccentrics, the mad gamblers, the miners, the storybook characters. It was very cosmopolitan. There were many Aborigines, Chinese and a lot of blow-ins from everywhere. And the big, orange Kimberley mountains surrounded the town. We loved it—and it changed us forever. The vastness, the ruggedness, the stillness, the stars, the breathtaking beauty—the landscape made you feel small and insignificant. All this and the incredible colours—blues and oranges, ochres and purples and grey-greens—were stored away in our subconscious to surface later in our present restaurant.

Balgo was like a small town with extremely well-designed buildings. There was a hospital, a school, living quarters, a chapel and a presbytery. It was a very impressive place which you wouldn't expect to find so far from civilisation. Big groups of the local tribe, the Gogadjas, camped near the compound. Balgo was run by a gregarious and imposing Palatine priest, Father Macguire, known as Father Mac, who was like a god to everyone. There was only one person Mac was terrified of, and that was Sister Frances, who ran the hospital and who later became famous for her remarkable work with lepers.

Mac was horrified by what he saw in the Kimberleys in the 1960s. He compared it to Britain's treatment of the Irish people—degrading and inhuman. His passionate ambition was to provide the Gogadjas with skills they could use to look after themselves, to teach their children and yet maintain their traditional ceremonies and rich cultural life.

There were a lot of wild brumbies around Balgo and Mac had horse-trainer friends in Victoria where he grew up. They thought the world of him and agreed to let him have some of the horses that were too old to race but had good lineage. One, Basin Street, had even entered the Melbourne Cup. Mac's idea was to cross them with the brumbies, build up a herd of stock horses and train the Aborigines to be stockmen. John also ran large numbers of cattle on the station. He built the first paddocks and brought in the first cattle. Eventually Balgo had some of the best stock horses and stockmen in the Kimberleys. When I went back two years ago I found that all my brother's stock boys either owned their own cattle stations or had top jobs on other stations.

I loved a special place near the mission called the Pound, where all the brumbies were held. It was on the site of an extinct inland sea and was at least thirty kilometres across—an amazing place of purple stone and crushed shells.

During that first stay Raymond did odd jobs on the mission and helped the nuns in the kitchen or the sewing room while my sister-in-law Norah and I helped in the school, where there were about 100 kids and only two teachers. Then I landed the job of stock camp cook. Our closest camp was approximately 200 kilometres from the mission, and we went out for weeks at a time, travelling with a few hundred head of cattle. It was like another planet out there in the desert—there were fragments of meteors all over the place and the vegetation was sparse, mostly spinifex. But it was thick with birds and the colours changed constantly.

I cooked breakfast, morning tea, lunch, afternoon tea and dinner for about twenty people, and the Aborigines ate this food with us. The conditions were primitive—just a small camp oven, a grill and half-a-dozen empty dried milk tins as improvised saucepans. The Gogadjas introduced us to native bush food, and their strong, distinctive flavours were like nothing we'd ever had before. They often cooked special things for themselves. They'd throw a goanna on the hot coals and when it was cooked they would slit open the skin and there would be this delicious sweet white flesh inside. Stunning! Or it

ABE KERSH

might be a snake. I had eaten a lot of eels growing up, so that didn't faze me at all. The Aboriginal stockmen would bring me gifts of food in their coolamons—bloodwood apples, akudjura or bush tomatoes, wild figs, bush tobacco and green, weedy things. Some were sweet, others were savoury or tart, which suited my palate; I'd been raised on soused and pickled fish. Raymond liked it too. But at that stage we didn't say, 'Oh, this is fantastic, we'll use it back home in our cooking.' It was just interesting and part of the desert experience.

I can't say the Aboriginal stockmen were equally appreciative of my cooking, though. Keen to bring variety to the basic camp diet of fresh beef, salted beef, damper and jam, I'd arrived armed with dried herbs and spices, including large quantities of garlic, chilli and cayenne pepper. After a week or two of moving cattle the head stockman, Tex, took my brother John aside and said: 'Ay, boss, Mr John's sister is queen of the camp but her tucker gives us the shits and a gut ache.'

From Balgo Raymond and I journeyed to Tasmania. There could be no greater contrast with the Kimberleys, but we revelled in the island's glorious produce and decidedly fresh approach to food, working at the Scotch Thistle Inn at Ross in the lush Midlands. Back in Sydney a year later we found ourselves working once again with our friend Woody, the chef from the Hotel Florida in Terrigal. Wherever he went, we went—Raymond as second chef and me front of house. In those days there were no credit cards and 99 per cent of the money received in restaurants was cash, so finding trustworthy staff was critical. Ray and I were honest and Woody knew it. And we were hard workers, and we loved what we were doing.

There were a lot of ups and downs in these years. In 1972 we ran a seafood restaurant with the hope of eventually becoming full partners. Cyren's was simple—mostly seafood, beautifully fried fish and chips and recipes supplied by the owner's Greek grandmother and

aunties. I left within a year when my back was injured in an accident at the restaurant, but Raymond stayed on. Abe and Edna and my sister Margaret all worked there and became very much involved with the life of our regular customers, a pattern that was to repeat itself at Edna's Table. After seven years and much success Raymond left too.

Ray and I didn't work together for a few years. I went to New Guinea, and it wasn't until my return to Australia that we talked seriously about having a restaurant of our own. I was determined that Raymond would never have to work so hard for someone else again, and that we should all be involved. Mum and Dad had long since divorced but were still great friends. Abe was retired and cirrhosis of the liver had severely curtailed his drinking habits. He was bored witless.

Through a friend we heard of someone who was looking to sub-let a restaurant in Kent Street. Raymond and I fell in love with the place. We had no money but we were going to make it work through sheer determination. We opened two weeks from the day we signed the lease, with Raymond and our great friend Gavin Cummings in the front kitchen, Abe and an apprentice in the back, Edna as telephonist and gofer, Margaret and me up front and a handpicked group of friends whom we had worked with on the floor. There was a great deal of work to do, but fortunately our friends helped us clean up. The electricity had been turned off for three months, and when we opened the cool room in the basement we reeled back. Inside were six whole cow carcasses—in a most unpleasant state. It had been an Argentinian restaurant and they cooked these beasts on a huge open barbecue in the centre of the restaurant.

Raymond decided that he wanted to put a kitchen in the barbecue area. Now, of course, there are dozens of open kitchens across Sydney, but in those days there was only one—La Grillade. The building inspector declared that it was impossible, whereupon Edna remembered that she had an old friend, Jackie Boyd, who headed up the Properties Department at the Sydney City Council. She went to see him, explaining that Raymond thought it would give a wonderful sense of theatre to have an open kitchen. Mum must have been persuasive, because we got it. It was like theatre in the round; the kitchen was the first thing you came into when you opened the door, and everyone sat around it. Even if people were having a bitch at one another or weren't enjoying each other's company, it didn't matter—they could always look at what was going on in the kitchen, which still had a mystique.

Raymond filled the restaurant with Australian decor, huge paintings of native birds and, just for fun, included a caricature of Abe—with beer gut, wrinkled T-shirt and trademark fag hanging from his mouth—which he stuck on the men's loo. We opened the doors on St Patrick's Day in 1981. It was an exciting time. We had only two weeks' rent in the bank. Mum and Dad were absolutely beside themselves.

Abe flourished at Edna's, and he couldn't have given us more at that stage in our lives. On the opening day Dad was in the back kitchen, and he virtually stayed there right up until a few months before he died. He trained all the young apprentices when they started and helped with all the tedious jobs that a restaurant is full of—the peeling and the washing and the cleaning. There wasn't a single apprentice chef who didn't end up admiring Abe. It was just like the old days when he was a foreign hand on 18-foot sailing boats—he never gave up, he worked until the end. Whether it was on a boat or in the back kitchen at Edna's Table, Abe never deserted, never jumped ship.

We had a wonderful kitchen hand called Charlie, a very tall, magnificent-bodied Maori, very handsome and very gay. He was on night shift at Christmas time not long before my father died. During the day the juicer had broken down and we'd sent it off to get fixed. It hadn't come back and we needed to squeeze a lot of limes. Charlie was flapping all round the kitchen asking

everyone what he was going to do. Abe was standing just outside with a cigarette hanging out of his mouth. 'We've got a new one, Charlie,' he said. 'We've got a new fruit juicer, it's the easiest one in the world. You don't even have to turn on the switch.' And Charlie said, 'Where is it, Abe?' Dad looked at Charlie and said, 'Haven't you heard about it? It's the new machine called the Armstrong, Charlie, your Armstrong fruit juicer.' Charlie wasn't all that bright and he said, 'But Abe, where is the Armstrong, where is it?' And Abe said, 'Charlie, it's there, hanging out of your shoulder, the arm strong.'

In the back of the restaurant Edna answered the phones, starched and ironed hundreds of doilies every day and helped Abe with the menial jobs like peeling the prawns. Margaret came to wait on tables and manage the bar. Stocking the bar was a problem, though, because our funds were so low. To make the place look good Raymond brought in from home his collection of exotic liqueur bottles that he'd been given over the years. But if anyone ordered something we didn't have, like Cointreau which was all the rage then, Edna had to slip out the back and go up to Sweeney's, the Irish pub on Druitt Street which had a bottle shop. The bar staff there said she wore a path between the two places in our first few weeks.

On the day we opened we said, 'Mum, the worst table in the restaurant is the table near the toilets.' It was table 17. 'This is your table; Edna's Table.' She thought it was wonderful and told us, 'Nothing will make me happier in the world than the day you ask me to go to the kitchen or the office to have my lunch, because that will be the day you are so busy, there won't be a spare table. That will make me smile, my kids with a full restaurant.'

It didn't take long for Edna to be moved regularly from her favourite table. One day when she was sitting at No. 17 with my aunties Phyllis, Ollie and Babin, I whizzed up and said, 'Mum, you've got to leave the table. Go out to the office. I'll tell the kitchen to send your grilled fish and chips out.' She could sense my urgency, and peered around to see who was coming to take her table. It was none other than the gorgeous, sexy Mel Gibson, with a film executive. My mother was thrilled to give up her table and even more thrilled when he ordered her favourite meal—soup of the day and grilled fish and chips.

When we opened Edna's Table Raymond had a vision that everyone could come and enjoy our food, not just the foodies. He was emphatic that there would always be a cold entree of prawns, there would always be grilled or deep-fried fish and chips, there would always be steak and chips and even side orders of chips. I didn't believe in this. The day we opened, Tony Bilson and Patric Juillet came to have lunch with us to show their support. They looked at the menu and said that if you were going to be taken seriously as a restaurant you wouldn't serve chips, you wouldn't just have char-grilled steak, and you certainly wouldn't serve a pie. Raymond's pies were masterpieces of invention—rabbit and hare with tarragon, goat with red wine and mushrooms. Raymond stuck to his belief that people wanted some simple things on the menu, dishes they felt comfortable with and weren't intimidated by. In the early days I disagreed with him, but I soon realised he was right. The crown of prawns was always up there as one of the best-selling entrees, the grilled fish and chips and the steak and chips sold as much as any other main course.

Although the location was then considered to be in the grubby end of town, as time went on we became successful. For nine years an amazing array of people came through our doors. There were politicians such as Bob Hawke, Gough Whitlam, Bill Hayden, John Hewson and John Howard. Other customers included Dawn Fraser, Ray Martin, Lisa Forrest, Kerri-Anne Kennerley, Anne Saunders, Margaret Whitlam, Tim Webster, Robin Williams, Sir Robert Helpmann, Stuart Challender, Jamie Packer, Larry Pickering, David Campese, Steve (Blocker) Roach, Benny Elias, Mark Ella, Pat O'Shane, Yvonne Goolagong Cawley, Graham Richardson, Min Keating,

Ann Keating, Stephen Loosley, Lady Mary Fairfax, Carla Zampatti, Ita Buttrose, John Singleton, Mike Carlton, Trevor Kennedy, John Newcombe, Des Renford, Jana Wendt, Max Walsh, Graham Kennedy and many others. Overseas celebrities came too—Billy Joel, Lee Remick, Sir Richard Attenborough, Norman Jewison, Leonie Mitchell and a constant stream of movie directors and producers. One unforgettable day we hosted a lunch Barry Humphries organised for Australian comedians.

We often had people from the film industry come to the restaurant. One Melbourne Cup day Peter Wilkinson, who ran Fox Columbia, rang and said that a lovely young actress called Sigourney Weaver was in town promoting a new film, and that she would be their guest of honour at a table for eighteen. Sigourney Weaver came, she saw, she wept and left. Our Melbourne Cup days were like great theatrical events, and as Abe had maintained several bookmakers financially during the course of his life this was appropriate. But for Sigourney it was culture clash on a grand scale. She found herself in a state of shock at the noise and the frenzied atmosphere, only slightly less frightening than a full-blown Los Angeles riot. Even though she won the sweep the significance of the event was lost on her, and she very graciously asked if she could leave. She wasn't used to lunching at restaurants where the patrons yelled across the tables—and not a security guard in sight! So she left, poor thing, looking as if she'd seen a ghost. Well, she was here to promote Ghostbusters.

Many of our regular customers became our friends, and the restaurant itself became an extension of our home. My niece Bianca and my nephew Rowan (a terror like his granddad Abe) grew up at Edna's Table, they had their birthdays there, and they were very much part of the restaurant. Many of Dad's old wharfie friends would come to the restaurant—they'd heard the news that Abe Kersh's kids had opened a restaurant in Kent Street. At one table

CARICATURES OF ABE AND EDNA FROM THE 1980S

you'd have playwright David Williamson, and at the next table there'd be three of Dad's old wharfie mates all ordering the most expensive wines, wharf wages having improved somewhat since my father's time.

After we'd been open a year or so, Gourmet magazine rang and said that they were going to include us in their list of recommendations. We were absolutely overwhelmed and surprised. We'd never sought the type of notice that goes with Gourmet Traveller or Vogue. The people from Gourmet wanted to know what we called the cuisine. I asked Raymond, and he said that obviously it was modern Australian. Today most of the top restaurants describe themselves as modern Australian, but back then the magazine informed us that there was no such thing, that one was influenced by French or Italian or some other cuisine. I have already mentioned Raymond's explosive temper; on this occasion he said, 'That's what we are. If you don't like it, don't put us in the book.' They chose to like it. At about the same time David Dale, the food writer and critic, gave the restaurant three out of four chef's hats. He described the restaurant as 'eclectic', and I suppose we still are.

All good things come to an end. The stock market crash of October 1987 was a severe blow to us. Abe and Edna had died within months of each other in 1984. I became very unwell and we had problems with the small print on our lease, which sent the rent up as fast as a rocket on the way out of the Earth's orbit. Sadly, on Christmas Eve 1989, we closed the doors on our beloved Edna's Table.

But we decided to try again. We still had the same passion to create a restaurant where people would feel at home and enjoy the experience, and we still had a passion for Australian native food which we'd previously been unable to channel for want of commercial suppliers. So we searched for a new position. Finally radio man and close friend Mike Carlton and his wife Kerry found us the site for Edna's Table II, in the heart of the conservative

CBD at the base of the MLC Tower. We're good at terrible locations; we have a wonderful knack for finding them. Though we made a success of it, there have been many times when we have thought that we should have opened a uniquely Australian restaurant in a less conservative part of town.

Raymond designed everything in the restaurant: the chairs, the lights, the Australian murals. We wanted to call the restaurant Narmaloo—the name of a special place, a waterhole at Balgo Hills. The Aborigines there had given us special permission for the name to be used, even though it was a sacred place. Ray and I felt it had such warm associations for us, and showed that we were serious about our Australian native food. It didn't occur to us that there would be a stumbling block. You can imagine our disbelief when we were told by the building's managers that we couldn't use that name—it was too 'ethnic'. This in Australia at the latter end of the 20th century! They tried to tell us politely that they wanted the same Edna's Table that had been at Kent Street, or something European, preferably French—an equally 'ethnic' proposal it seemed to me. So Edna's Table it was.

But the old name remains a good one. By an extraordinary coincidence, the person who was numbering the tables in the new restaurant placed No. 17 right next to the toilets. It set me thinking about Edna, and when I recalled her own connection with the Kimberleys I realised that it was right to keep her name.

I'll always remember when Mum came back from her trip to Balgo. She'd been away for three months so we talked endlessly about everything that had happened. She loved the Gogadja people and she thought the nuns at the mission station were wonderful, but it surprised her that some of the white people didn't have any warmth with the Aboriginal people. Because she came from Pyrmont and was uneducated but very sensitive to snobbery, she

LEMON MYRTLE BAVAROIS COATED IN WILD LIME JELLY PG **153**

noticed all there was to see. There wasn't anything that could escape Edna in her very quiet, dignified way.

She told me the story of Munja who used to do the gardening. Munja was a very elegant, colourful Gogadja woman who spoke reasonable English. Whenever the anthropologists came to Balgo, which was frequently because the Gogadja are said to have the oldest skull formation in the world, she managed to mesmerise and charm all of them. She used to look after the garden and help my sister-in-law by minding and playing with the two little boys, Sean and Matthew. She was very sensitive to Mum and they were great mates. Mum would make scones for her and they'd have afternoon tea.

One day they were sitting there at the table and a nun arrived from the mission. She took one look, asked Mum to step outside and said, 'Mrs Kersh, we don't do that.' Mum said, 'Don't do what?' The nun said, 'Er, with Munja, you know, Mrs Kersh.' And Mum told me that she just looked at her and said, 'Why?' The nun got flustered, told Edna she didn't understand and just went back in a huff to the main mission.

All Mum said was, 'Why?' And perhaps what Raymond and I are saying today, about the food produced by this great continent, is simply, 'Why not?'

People most probably think it's unusual for a brother and sister to work together for thirty-three years. Some brothers might think that working with a sister is a life sentence. For Raymond I'm sure it has been—he has my sympathy. I'm an extraordinarily demanding human being when it comes to food and detail.

What's more I am amazingly prone to having accidents at the worst possible times for him.

John Cleese once said that farce is what happens to you on the worst day of your life, and I often feel I've lived out scenes from a Fawlty Towers script. I tend to run about at

GUINEA FOWL ON KUMARA AND PARSNIP GALLETTES WITH PARCELS PG 106

great speed when I'm working, and the faster I run the more fuel I need. One evening in the restaurant at about ten o'clock I realised I had completely forgotten to eat—it had been a very busy night. I dashed through the kitchen and found our young chef had one quail left over. I was busy wolfing it when someone informed me that I was urgently required elsewhere, so with one mighty gulp I swallowed the lot. Fifteen minutes later I was in trouble. Raymond was always telling me that I should eat more slowly, so I couldn't bring myself to tell him that I seemed to be choking to death on a very busy night—I just slipped off to the Sydney Hospital Emergency Department. In the absence of an ear, nose and throat specialist, I was assured that I had only suffered bruising of the throat and that I should go home. Unfortunately I didn't improve overnight, and by noon the following day I was back in hospital, being rushed into surgery. As I was being wheeled into the theatre a nurse rushed up saying that there was someone on the phone with a very important message. It was Raymond. 'Jennice,' he barked, 'who have you got on for lunch? We have ninety bookings—have you got enough staff?' I replied from my slab that I was about to undergo an operation, and he said, 'Well, that's right, because you're careless, aren't you!' The operation was a success, fortunately for me. The doctors even presented me with the offending quail bone, which I kept and subsequently had put into a piece of jewellery hoping that it would cure me from eating on the run.

It didn't, of course. Only three weeks after we'd opened Edna's Table II, I ate a piece of fish on the run and I again got The Glare from Raymond as I was carted off to Sydney Hospital for yet another operation. I remember thinking that I really should learn to eat more slowly.

I should also learn to move more slowly. One day at the end of 1995, I was scrambling through the restaurant in my high heels, hoping to have a bite to eat before the six o'clock pre-Phantom of the Opera dinner rush. We'd kept some Moroccan-style chicken with ratatouille and lemon aspen dressing for that night's staff meal, where we were to farewell Lesley-Anne, whom we all loved. I threw the biggest serve of ratatouille over the chicken, and was running out the kitchen door when I tripped and dropped the plate. Somehow I managed to ski across it and slam into the wall. When I came to, I was sitting there covered in ratatouille, with a large plastic drum of washing-up detergent inexplicably lodged between my legs. I had also broken my arm and three ribs. Raymond came out. There was The Glare. 'I cannot believe that she doesn't sit and eat like a proper human being,' he said, and returned to the kitchen. I made yet another trip to see my friends at Sydney Hospital, where rumour has it I now fill a filing cabinet of accident records.

Fortunately for us all, Raymond is good in an emergency. He has the energy of six people—I have never seen anyone produce as much as Ray—the modesty and generosity of a saint, and to work with him is an absolute inspiration. He's not bound by structure, and he attributes that to the fact that he's dyslexic. We grew up in a family where there were no cookbooks, and Ray couldn't have read them even if we had them. Many chefs I know love reading cookbooks. They're consumed by them! Ray will find some new native ingredient, look at it, taste it, experiment with it to create some new flavour or combination of flavours. He's always had style and artistry in whatever he does, whether it's cooking, sewing or design. In some ways Raymond has brought his love of sewing to his food; throughout this book there are recipes in parcels or wrapping—that's the tailor at work.

In this business even the most creative people have bad days—don't believe them if they say otherwise. Once, back in 1982, Raymond was asked by one of our customers if he could make a 21st birthday cake for her daughter, who loved French history and had been studying Marie Antoinette. Raymond's cakes were always an event; he didn't just decorate them, he turned out three-dimensional sculptures that were a pity to eat—they should have been on display in an art gallery. On this special occasion, Raymond spent two days making a full-length sculpture cake of Marie Antoinette dressed in pink and decorated to the nines. We put it in the cool room. Just before the dinner was about to be served to the 110 guests, a waiter went down to the cool room, slipped, and dropped a whole case of champagne on poor Marie, who lost her head for the second time. She was beyond recognition—a sea of pink goo. Raymond was just not destined to produce anything French. None of the guests was aware of the drama except for Carol Allen, the understanding mother and hostess, but it was one of the worst moments in Raymond's cooking career.

We have had many great days, though, particularly our annual celebrations of St Patrick's Day, the Melbourne Cup and Christmas. For St Patrick's Day we have our own book of songs, from 'I'll Take You Home Again Kathleen' to 'Hail Queen of Heaven' to 'Danny Boy'. We sing 'Jerusalem' and dedicate it to Abe.

Christmas was Edna's special time. She used to give everyone a present—from favourite customers to the local SP bookmaker, the nuns, every third and fourth cousin. It was on Christmas Eve that my mother had her last, fatal heart attack. She'd had very bad chest pains all day and hadn't told anyone. She'd come home and had begun to wrap twenty-five or thirty of her Christmas cakes as presents. In the middle of all this the pain became too much to bear, and the ambulance arrived to take her to hospital. It turned out she'd had a heart attack and she died a few days later. The thing that stands out in my mind is that when she was taken off to hospital she was busy wrapping gifts for people. She had just written the words 'To Singo' on a card for our good friend, advertising chief John Singleton. The next year we didn't think we could face Christmas again, but instead we made it our most special night, a night of families, of food, of

ST PATRICK'S DAY IN THE 1980S:
MICHAEL CLEARY, JENNICE AND MICHAEL BAILEY

children and giving, a night that Edna would have been proud of.

I have always been as passionate as Raymond in appreciating the magnificent native produce we have in this country. Fortunately we are becoming increasingly proud of what we can produce—in food, wine, literature, film. In the early 1980s, for instance, you would sell not only a great amount of French champagne, but also of French wine. If someone wanted to impress a client, out came the French wine. By the time we closed the old Edna's Table in 1989, you would be lucky to sell one bottle of French wine, other than champagne, every three months. The change was extraordinary, and now it extends to our foods as well.

When we started working with native foods in Sydney, many thought it a daring, bold venture, but never once did we feel we should change tack. Sometimes we've felt like native plants ourselves—we go through fire and come out regenerated. There have been times when I've been impatiently wishing that everyone else would hurry up and appreciate what magnificent produce this Australian native food is. It's not just a trend, it's part of our culture. The Aborigines and the food of our land are part of our identity. When we opened the present Edna's Table the twelve ingredients we could get regularly included lemon myrtle, Illawarra plum, Tasmanian pepperberry, pepperleaf, lemon aspen, quandong, riberry and munthari berry. It wasn't long before we realised that Australians were afraid of these ingredients, so we decided to put them on the table along with bottles of oil flavoured with native herbs. We had some little coolamons from the Northern Territory and we hit on the idea of putting the bush tomato, pepperberries and so on in them. The more Ray cooked with these flavours, the more excited I got because I could see the potential. Slowly people began to take notice. We found we were filling up the coolamons on the table more often and

more and more of our clients were listening to their palates, and coming to recognise foods that are growing all around us.

One of our very good customers is John Bell, from the Abbott Tout law firm in the MLC Centre. He also owns a property in the country at Canowindra. One lunchtime he ordered charcoal fillet of beef with Tasmanian pepperberry jus and potato rosti. He said that he loved the pepperberry. Now, at the time we happened to be helping to promote World Environment for the Mount Annan Botanic Gardens in Narellan, New South Wales. Mount Annan was a present to the people of New South Wales for the Bicentenary in 1988, given to us by the government, with 800 hectares dealing only in native flowers and plants. I had a display of some native fruit-bearing trees in the foyer of the restaurant. I went over to the display and got some pepperberry to show John. He took one look at the deep emerald leaves and the lavender berry and nearly fell off his chair. 'Jennice,' he said, 'I can't believe it. I had these growing all over my property. Now we've cleared the land and we've planted olive trees everywhere. We pull the branches off the Tasmanian pepperberry and give them to the sheep.'

Often on a Sunday I have a long telephone conversation with my brother John who now lives in far north-west Queensland. A couple of months ago he mentioned that while he was out checking the fences in the far paddock he had found a few dead sheep. He was cursing the drought that so often afflicts our country, and then briefly mentioned that nearby he had found some of my favourite bush cucumbers. 'Oh,' he said, 'they were growing everywhere. I brought some in and I'll send them to you in a postpak.' I laughed. 'John, doesn't that tell you something? The sheep are dead but those bloody bush cucumbers are alive and doing well without any help!' There has to be a simple message here.

Recently I spoke at a conference on Emerging Opportunities in Agriculture in New South Wales, put together by an inspiring man, Dr Michael Burke from the Australian National University. After many years specialising in the agricultures and indigenous foods of the South Pacific, he realised that he had no idea about our wonderful indigenous foods and thought others should hear about them too. Some 600 farmers came to the conference. The session on native Australian ingredients was a tremendous success with delegates coming up afterwards seeking more information—a small but important step on the path to greater understanding of the old foods of this ancient land.

We have an opportunity to develop these old flavours, the foods that have been growing here for thousands of years. Why not welcome them and mix them with the modern style? Native pepperberry-flavoured olive oil, for instance, or lemon myrtle olive oil. I believe the greatest challenge lies ahead—to start farming Australian native foods and creating an exciting new food industry. For instance, there are twenty different types of bush tomato in this country; they're very strong and robust in flavour, but as small as a grape. Imagine if we crossed them with a Roma and all that lovely flavour went into a big lush tomato.

Talented young cooks have developed an exciting, multicultural modern Australian cuisine, and flavours which twenty years ago were considered exotic have become part of our daily diet. They are also part of what tourists seek when visiting this country. It's surely time for us to enrich this cuisine with the flavours of our own land.

Foreign food writers and journalists specifically ask to eat at our restaurant when they visit Australia. They love the food and go back and write articles praising it to the skies. The hottest food magazine in Italy, Slow Food, has sent writers to investigate Australian food in depth. The US edition of Newsweek has given us favourable mention. We've had about twenty-five overseas television organisations come to film what we do, and endless magazine and newspaper articles about our food. But in Australia, most of the leading chefs and food writers ignore native herbs and spices—except for a token use here and there—and yet the herbs and spices they do use are indigenous to other lands.

The great Australian cook and food writer Margaret Fulton told me when she first visited the new Edna's Table that she had to be honest but she didn't like native food or 'bush tucker'. She was there because her friends wanted to try it. However, she ordered two entrees to be polite. Halfway through the second one, she sent for me. 'Jennice,' she said, 'I've had flavours here today I've never had before and it's very exciting. When he's finished in the kitchen, could Raymond come and sit with me for a while?' Raymond, who adores and respects Margaret, came as soon as he was free and we sat talking for a couple of hours. Finally she said to us, 'You have a very important message to tell Australia. I don't care if you never make a cent, but you have to write a cookbook.' And this from the woman who changed Australia's eating habits forever when she made European food acceptable to average people back in the 1960s.

So we've taken Margaret's advice and hope that it helps Australians embrace and enjoy the food and flavours of their land. Just think about it: one day our children will take sandwiches to school filled with warrigal greens, kangaroo prosciutto and wild Davidson plum chutney. In doing so they will be eating the food of our indigenous people and showing respect for them on the simplest level of all—their everyday diet.

Raymond and I have a dream that one day adventurous farmers in Western Australian and North Queensland will work together with Aboriginal people to create a great local and export food industry. I can think of no better way to further the process of reconciliation.

S

O U P S

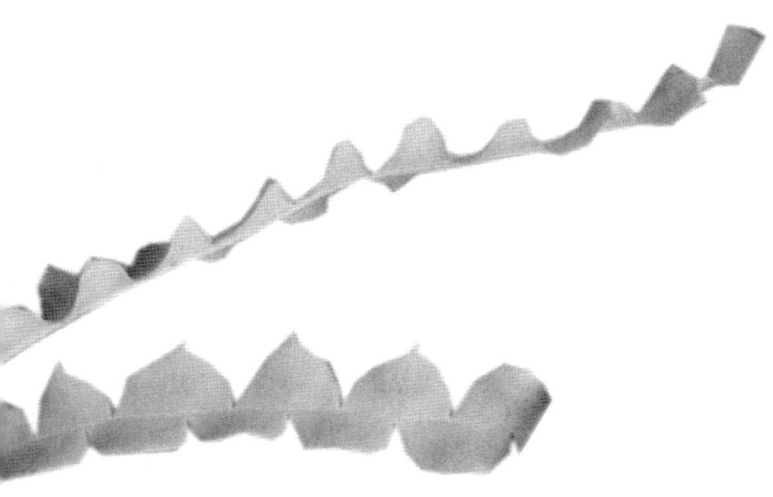

CHILLED SUGAR SNAP PEA AND NATIVE ANISEED SOUP

My aunties, Annie, Babbin, Ollie and Dorrie all lived near Mum in Pyrmont. They would sit around Edna's table and shell fresh peas, bought fresh that day from Alf the fruitman. My mother never wore an apron but my aunts did—lovely, big crispy ironed ones. They'd peel the peas into the apron and throw the shells to the side. They drank endless cups of tea and ate Edna's wonderful scones in our kitchen. This scene is an enduring memory of my childhood.

Serves 6–8

2 litres fish stock	1 x 2.5 cm knob ginger, roughly chopped
1 onion, roughly chopped	200 g butter
1 leek, roughly chopped	1 kg sugar snap peas, topped and tailed
1 stick celery, roughly chopped	1 tablespoon native aniseed
1 chilli, de-seeded and chopped	200 g natural yoghurt
3 cloves garlic, roughly chopped	salt and pepper, to taste

Bring the fish stock to the boil in a saucepan over low heat. While the fish stock is heating, sauté the onion, leek, celery, chilli, garlic and ginger in the butter in a separate pan. When they are softened and fragrant, add the snap peas and sauté for 1–2 minutes until warmed through. Add the boiling fish stock and boil for 1–2 minutes. Remove from the heat, purée and strain through a sieve.

When cool, stir the native aniseed and the yoghurt through, season to taste and chill in the refrigerator. Serve cold.

TOMATO AND NATIVE MINT SOUP

Serves 6–8

2 1/2 kg Roma (egg-shaped) tomatoes	2 tablespoons native mint
salt and pepper, to taste	600 ml chicken stock
6 whole cloves garlic, skin on	cream and native mint, extra, to garnish

Arrange the tomatoes on a baking tray, and sprinkle with salt and pepper and the whole garlic cloves. Roast at 150°C for about 1 hour or until they are very soft but not blackened or burnt.

Remove the garlic cloves, peel them, then purée with the tomatoes. Strain the purée into a saucepan and add the native mint and chicken stock. Bring to the boil, stirring well.

Serve immediately with a swirl of cream and a pinch of native mint.

PARSNIP AND BUSH TOMATO (AKUDJURA) SOUP

We were camped at Middleton's Bore on Balgo Station in the Kimberleys, and I was the stock camp cook. One of the Aboriginal stockmen, Tex, brought me a handful of bush tomatoes (Akudjura) which they had dried in the sun. I bit into one expecting a lovely soft fruit, only to discover a texture more like a granite marble. My front tooth broke off, leaving me looking like the Wild Witch of the West for the next couple of weeks—there weren't any dentists to rescue female vanity in Balgo!

Serves 6–8

1 onion, roughly chopped

3 cloves garlic, roughly chopped

5 tablespoons bush tomato

750 g parsnips, roughly chopped

250 g potatoes, roughly chopped

150 g butter

2 litres beef, chicken or vegetable stock

salt and pepper, to taste

Sauté the onion, garlic, bush tomato, parsnips and potatoes in the butter until all the ingredients are well softened. Add the stock, bring to the boil, then reduce the heat and simmer for 10–15 minutes or until the potatoes are well cooked.

Remove the soup from the heat, purée, season to taste and strain back into the saucepan. The soup should be returned to the heat before serving.

CHILLED WATERCRESS AND PEPPERMINT SOUP

Serves 8

2 litres fish stock

1 onion, roughly chopped

1 leek, roughly chopped

1 stick celery, roughly chopped

1 chilli, roughly chopped

3 cloves garlic, roughly chopped

1 x 2.5 cm knob ginger, roughly chopped

150 g butter

250 g potatoes, peeled and evenly diced

1 1/2 bunches watercress, stems removed

2 tablespoons native peppermint

200 g natural yoghurt

Place the fish stock in a saucepan and cook over low heat. Meanwhile, in a separate large saucepan, sauté the onion, leek, celery, chilli, garlic and ginger in the butter.

Bring the fish stock to the boil, then pour it over the sautéed vegetables with the potatoes. Simmer steadily for about 15 minutes, or until the potato is well cooked. Add the watercress and peppermint, simmer for 2 minutes, then remove from the heat.

Purée, strain and cool, then mix in the yoghurt thoroughly. Serve chilled.

LEMON MYRTLE PRAWN BISQUE

My first memory of prawns is on a Friday when my Grandmother Florrie would come down from Carramar. Dad always went to the markets to get special things like baby school prawns, because Nanna Florrie was a favourite of his. Meanwhile I'd go up to Conlon's bakery—Mr Conlon would let me help him pull the bread from the oven and then I'd take it straight home, hot and delicious. Mum and Dad and Nanna would be there peeling the prawns, Dad would make fresh mayonnaise and we'd squeeze fresh lemons over them too. It was all such a ritual.

Dad always bought extra prawns and he'd make Nanna's favourite, an Indian-style prawn curry. If there weren't many prawns, he'd make a Chinese-style prawn and vegetable omelette, which was my sister Margaret's favourite dish.

Serves 8

4 cloves garlic, roughly chopped

1 x 4 cm knob ginger, roughly chopped

1 chilli, roughly chopped

1 onion, roughly chopped

1 leek, roughly chopped

1 carrot, roughly chopped

1 stick celery, roughly chopped

2 tablespoons lemon myrtle

150 g butter

3 kg prawn heads and shells

6 lemon myrtle leaves

3 tablespoons tomato paste

3 litres water

350 ml tomato juice

salt and pepper, to taste

1 lime juiced

Sauté the garlic, ginger, chilli, onion, leek, carrot, celery and lemon myrtle in the butter for about 5 minutes or until softened and fragrant. Add the prawn shells and heads, lemon myrtle leaves and tomato paste and sauté for a further 5 minutes. Add the water and tomato juice, bring to the boil, then reduce the heat and simmer for 1 hour.

Remove from the heat and purée the mixture including the heads and shells. Strain well, then return to the saucepan and cook over low heat until reduced by about half.

Season to taste, add lime juice and serve.

PYRMONT

KANGAROO TAIL BROTH

Serves 8

STOCK:

2 kg kangaroo tails

1 leek, roughly chopped

1 brown onion, roughly chopped

2 carrots, roughly chopped

1 stick celery, roughly chopped

olive oil

1 cup red wine

3 tablespoons tomato paste

4 litres water

FOR THE SOUP:

2 tablespoons redcurrant jelly

1 leek, finely chopped

1 brown onion, finely chopped

2 medium carrots, finely chopped

1 stick celery, finely chopped

4 cloves garlic

3 tablespoons butter

TO MAKE THE STOCK, roast the kangaroo tails in a baking dish at 180°C for about 45 minutes, or until the meat starts to fall from the bone. In a stockpot or large saucepan, sauté the leek, onion, carrots and celery in the oil. When the vegetables are fragrant and beginning to soften, add the kangaroo tails, red wine, tomato paste and water, bring to the boil, then reduce the heat to a bare simmer and cook, uncovered, for 4 hours. Keep an eye on the stock, and top it up with a little water if the liquid level drops below the bones. Remove from the heat and strain, reserving the bones. There should be about 4 litres of stock.

TO MAKE THE SOUP, simmer the strained stock until it has reduced by half. Pick the meat from the kangaroo tail bones, chop it roughly and add it to the broth with the redcurrent jelly.

Sauté the leek, onion, carrots, celery and garlic in the butter until well softened, and add this mixture to the broth. Bring to the boil, season to taste and serve.

KANGAROO CONSOMME

Serves 8

150 g minced kangaroo meat

6 egg whites

1 stick celery, roughly chopped

2 carrots, roughly chopped

1 onion, roughly chopped

8–10 sprigs of thyme

2 bay leaves

10 peppercorns

2 cloves garlic

3 litres cold Kangaroo Stock (see recipe page 170)

Combine the kangaroo mince, egg whites, celery, carrots, onion, thyme, bay leaves, peppercorns and garlic in a mixing bowl.

Place the kangaroo stock in a large saucepan with the mince and egg white mixture and bring slowly to the boil. Stir occasionally. The egg whites should form a layer at the surface of the liquid.

Reduce the heat till the liquid is at a bare simmer and cook for up to 3 hours, uncovered, without stirring so that the egg white layer is not disturbed during this time.

The consommé is ready when the liquid is clear and strongly flavoured. Test for this by scooping a little liquid from the edges of the pot with a ladle or large spoon. When you are satisfied with the flavour, remove all of the liquid with a ladle or large spoon, still taking care not to break the egg layer, and pour it through a strainer covered with a piece of fine muslin into another saucepan. Discard the egg white.

Before serving, reheat gently without boiling.

STA
TE

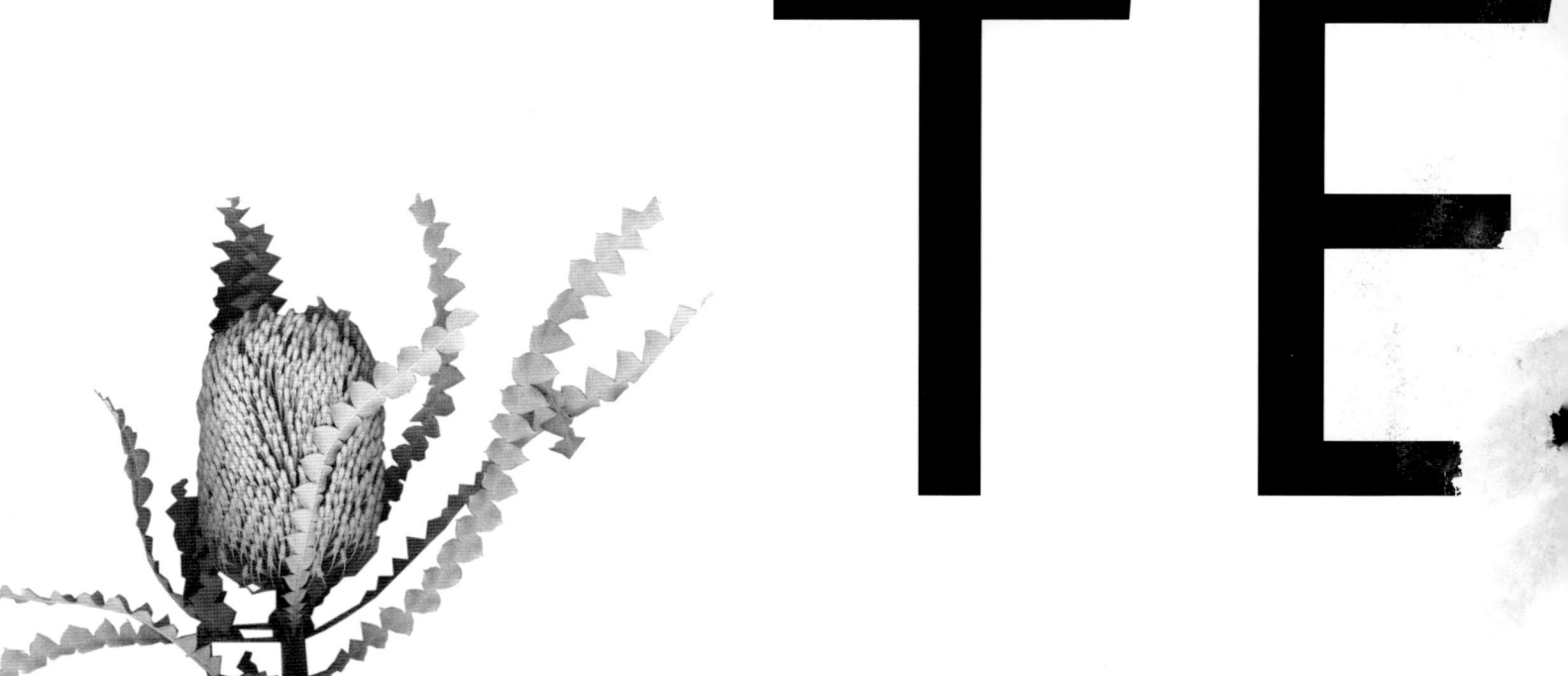

R

RS

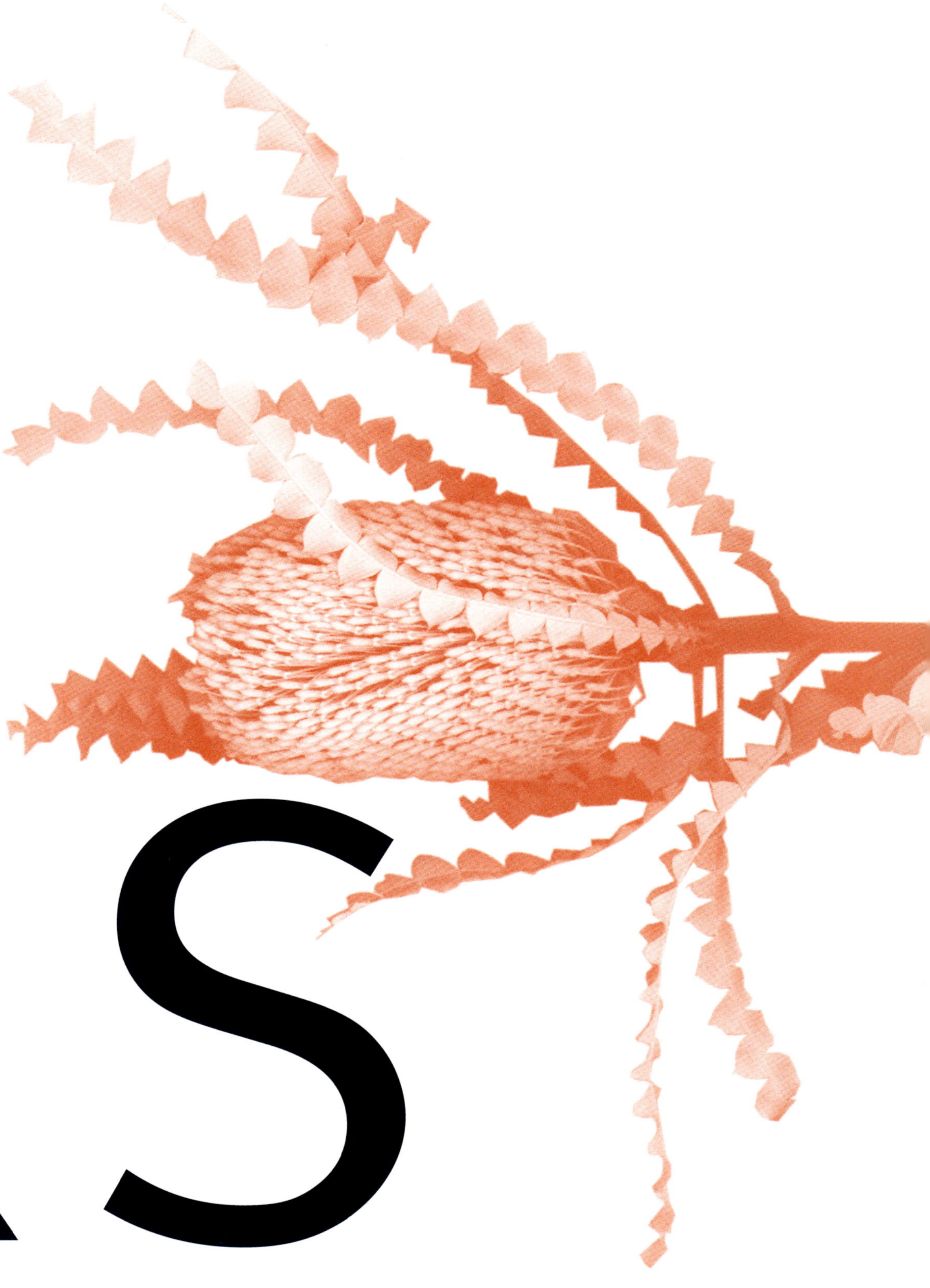

OYSTERS

SAFFRON AND NATIVE ANISEED DIPPING SAUCE

1 tablespoon native aniseed	1 nip (30 ml) ouzo
1 medium onion, finely chopped	500 ml cream
25 g butter	small pinch saffron
150 ml dry white wine	100 g butter, extra
100 ml white wine vinegar	salt and pepper, to taste

Sauté the aniseed and onion in a saucepan in the butter for 4–5 minutes or until fragrant. Add the white wine, white wine vinegar and ouzo, bring to the boil and cook until reduced by three-quarters, stirring occasionally. Add the cream and saffron and cook until reduced again by three-quarters, stirring occasionally.

Place the sauce in a blender and slowly blend in the extra butter, adding small pieces one at a time. Season to taste.

Serve in ramekins as a dipping sauce with fresh oysters in the shell, or drizzle over the oysters on a plate.

WARRIGAL GREENS AND MACADAMIA NUT PESTO

1/2 cup roasted macadamia nuts	1/2 bunch fresh basil leaves, stems removed
1/2 cup parmesan cheese, grated	salt and pepper, to taste
1 1/2 cups olive oil	2 tablespoons pink peppercorns
2 cups fresh warrigal greens	

Purée the macadamia nuts, parmesan and 1/4 cup of the oil in a blender. Add the warrigal greens, basil, parmesan cheese and remaining oil, season to taste and blend to a grainy paste.

To serve, top each oyster with a teaspoon of the pesto, and garnish with a pair of pink peppercorns.

Makes 2 1/2 cups or enough pesto for 6 dozen oysters. The pesto will keep in a sealed jar in the refrigerator for up to 4 weeks.

OYSTERS AND CRACKED PEPPERBERRY CREME FRAICHE WITH OCEAN TROUT ROE PG 57

CHEESEFRUIT DIPPING SAUCE

50 ml cheesefruit juice	1/2 cup cream
125 g Tallegio cheese, roughly chopped	1 teaspoon turmeric
60 g blue cheese, roughly chopped	1/4 fresh pineapple, skin and core removed and cut into chunks
(e.g. King Island or Stilton)	60 ml fish stock or water
1 clove garlic, finely chopped	salt and pepper, to taste

Place the cheesefruit juice, cheeses, garlic, cream and turmeric in a saucepan and cook over low heat, stirring occasionally to help combine.

Meanwhile, purée the pineapple and fish stock in a blender then add to the cheese mixture, stir through and cook, simmering, for about 20 minutes. Season to taste, strain through a fine sieve and cool.

Serve as a dipping sauce on each plate, or place in a number of ramekins around a large platter of oysters.

Makes 2 1/2 cups or enough sauce for 6 dozen oysters. The sauce will keep in a sealed jar in the refrigerator for 1 week.

CRACKED PEPPERBERRY CREME FRAICHE WITH OCEAN TROUT ROE

- 2 teaspoons cracked pepperberries
- 1 cup crème fraîche
- 100 g ocean trout roe, or other large pink or orange fish roe

Beat the pepperberries through the crème fraîche.

To serve, place a scant teaspoon of the créme fraîche mixture onto each oyster, and top with 1/2 teaspoon of ocean trout roe.

Makes enough for 6 dozen oysters. The mixture will keep in a sealed container in the refrigerator for up to 2 weeks (depending on the use-by date of the crème fraîche).

SALMON TARTARE PG **83**

oysters

Every Sunday in summer we used to go and watch Dad and his mates sail the 18-footers. If the weather wasn't good, we'd go out on the ferry and watch the race. The ferry would pick up the punters at Pyrmont, who would then place their bets on the various boats. There was beer, and cheese and Jatz crackers—they had to have food to legally sell the beer. There was nothing for kids, just water, but we loved watching Dad sail. Later on, we'd go on my Uncle Jack's small wooden boat, the 'Old Duck'.

If it was a fine day we'd go to Nielsen Park and have a big picnic. We'd arrive early in the morning and come home really, really late, after sundown. Mum would have us four children and two or three other kids with her. We'd catch the bus into town and get the ferry to Nielsen Park, where she would set up the picnic in a little pergola. When it was time for the race we'd go up to the western headland and watch.

While we waited for Dad's boat we'd sit on the rocks and pick at the oysters. My brothers had penknives and would prise the oysters open, and the wonderful flavour of the sea is as fresh in my mind today as when we were children.

CUCUMBER AND DRIED BUSH TOMATO DIPPING SAUCE

1 telegraph cucumber

150 ml dry white wine

2 tablespoons dried bush tomato

1 tablespoon oil

1 cup Light Mayonnaise (see recipe page 158)

salt and pepper, to taste

Roughly chop three-quarters of the cucumber and place in a saucepan with the white wine. Cook at a strong simmer until the wine has almost evaporated, leaving the cucumber softened and very moist. Purée the cucumber in a blender.

Fry the bush tomato in the oil until lightly browned—this will enhance the tomato's flavour.

Blend the puréed cucumber with the bush tomato and mayonnaise and stir through the remaining cucumber, diced into 1 cm cubes. Season to taste.

Serve in little ramekins with the oysters.

WILD LIME AND VODKA DRESSING

1/4 cup whole wild limes

small tub of ice cubes

1 fresh lime, juiced

1 nip vodka

1 cup Light Mayonnaise (see recipe page 158)

To remove the bitter flavour from the limes, bring a small saucepan of water to the boil, drop in the limes, remove immediately then plunge in iced water. Repeat.

Combine the lime juice, vodka and mayonnaise in a bowl. Finely chop the limes and add to the bowl.

Drizzle the dressing over the oysters on a plate, or serve separately as a dipping sauce.

Makes enough dressing for 6 1/2 dozen oysters. The dressing will keep in a sealed jar in the refrigerator for 2 weeks.

SCALLOPS IN THE SHELL WITH TROPICAL WILD LIME AND LIMONCELLO LIQUEUR

2 cups warrigal greens or English spinach	1/4 cup wild limes blanched in boiling water
24 scallops, on the shell	2 nips (1/4 cup) Limoncello liqueur
4 cups fish stock	vegetable oil
1 chilli, de-seeded and finely chopped	salt and pepper, to taste
juice and zest of 1 lime	4 tablespoons continental parsley, finely chopped
1 tablespoon brown sugar	

Blanch the warrigal greens. Remove the scallops from the shells and set the scallops aside. Place the shells on a flat baking tray and cover each with a small portion of the blanched greens to form a little bed.

Combine the fish stock, chilli, lime juice and zest and sugar in a small saucepan. Bring to the boil and cook until the liquid has reduced by half. Add the wild limes and Limoncello and remove from the heat. Keep warm.

Bake the scallop shells and greens at 150°C for 5 minutes or until just heated through. Meanwhile, sear the scallops in a lightly oiled, hot frying pan for about 2 minutes, turning once or twice. Take care not to overcook the scallops as they should be served rare and tender. Season to taste and sprinkle with the parsley.

Place the scallops onto the pre-heated shells and greens and spoon over the warm sauce.

Both the shells and sauce can be prepared shortly ahead of time and heated through just as the scallops are seared. Serve on a large, communal platter, or set out on individual plates at a more formal meal.

Serves 6 as a starter, or allow 2 scallops per person for finger food.

SEARED DUCK LIVERS WITH NATIVE THYME AND ILLAWARRA PLUM SALSA

Duck livers always remind us of Chez George, a stunning restaurant in Philip Street, Sydney on the site of the present Intercontinental Hotel. George was the owner-chef, a charming, delightfully mad Polish Jew. He was always dressed to perfection and heavily laden with expensive rings, presents from the Aga Khan (George had been his personal chef). George had also been in a German concentration camp during World War II. Every night after kitchen service, George would play the grand piano for his guests. The restaurant was like its owner: warm and stylish with wonderful food—especially the duck livers.

Mum and Ray gave my brother John a very elegant 21st birthday dinner at Chez George. We were having such a good time, dancing and drinking till the early hours; Edna could see that more expensive wine was being drunk than she and Ray had saved for. She slipped out to see George in the kitchen, who told her not to worry: she should enjoy the evening and pay later when she was able. Edna was at that time the cleaning lady for the ABC Drama Department. Every pay day for weeks afterwards she would trot down to Chez George and, over some delicious continental cakes, pay another instalment.

Serves 6

1/4 cup plain flour

24 duck livers, trimmed

1 teaspoon garlic, finely chopped

2 tablespoons Garlic and Ginger Oil
(see recipe page 158)

1 teaspoon dried native thyme

1 teaspoon native pepperleaf

1 pinch salt

1 tablespoon brandy

4 loose cups baby watercress or similar greens

Illawarra Plum Salsa (see recipe page 161)

Lightly flour the duck livers. Fry the garlic in the oil until just fragrant—be careful not to overcook. Add the duck livers to the pan and sear until just pink. Add the thyme, pepperleaf and salt and toss through. Add the brandy, increase the heat and flame the brandy—cook for 1 minute. Remove from the heat.

Serve on a bed of baby watercress, drizzled with the Illawarra Plum Salsa.

SEAFOOD AND PALMASAMI PARCELS WITH BUSH TOMATO SAUCE

Serves 6

1 tablespoon garlic, finely chopped

1 tablespoon ginger, finely chopped

2 tablespoons oil

1 leek, washed and finely sliced

12 silver beet leaves, stems removed, blanched and patted dry

3 sheets compressed, roasted seaweed (used for sushi and available in sheets from Asian food stores)

1/3 cup Palmasami (see recipe page 165)

12 medallions lobster meat or 12 green king prawns, shelled

12 large Tasmanian scallops

Bush Tomato Sauce (see recipe page 162)

Fry the garlic and ginger gently in the oil until just fragrant—do not overcook. Add the leeks and sweat through until just softened. Set aside to cool.

Cut each sheet of seaweed into 4 even strips and lay out the silver beet leaves ready for wrapping up the parcels. In the centre of each leaf place 1 teaspoon of palmasami, 1 teaspoon of the leek mixture, 1 lobster medallion or prawn and 1 scallop.

To make the parcels, fold the leaves firmly around the filling to form a neat parcel, dampen the ends of the seaweed strips and roll one around each parcel to hold it closed, pressing the damp end of the strip on firmly to secure.

Bake the parcels on a lightly oiled tray at 180°C for 5 minutes or until the seafood is just cooked through.

Serve with Bush Tomato Sauce.

BABY EGGPLANT STUFFED WITH CRAB AND MUSSELS

2 leeks, finely chopped

1 stick celery, finely chopped

1 tablespoon garlic, finely chopped

1 tablespoon ginger, finely chopped

2 tablespoons fresh mint, chopped

1/2 tablespoon native mint

2 tablespoons oil

200 g cooked crab meat

200 g mussels, shells removed, cooked, cleaned and sliced

salt and pepper, to taste

9 baby eggplants

1/4 cup milk

1 egg

1 cup plain flour

1 cup breadcrumbs

olive oil

Fry the leeks, celery, garlic and ginger in the oil over a low heat until sweating. Remove from the heat and add the crab meat, mussels, fresh mint, native mint and season to taste. Combine gently.

Cut the eggplants in half lengthwise, then slit a central pocket along the length of the exposed flesh of each half, taking care not to let the knife cut through to the outer skin. Fill the pockets with the cooked mixture.

Beat milk and egg together. Crumb each eggplant by coating in plain flour then the egg mixture, allowing the excess to drip off, then rolling in breadcrumbs. Deep fry in oil for about 4 minutes or until golden brown, or arrange on a lightly greased oven tray and bake at 180°C for about 15 minutes or until lightly browned.

For finger food, serve with a dipping sauce such as sweet chilli or Lemon Myrtle Hollandaise (see recipe page 167). As a starter, serve with Pandana Leaf Sauce (see recipe page 161).

Serves 6 as a starter, or allow 1 per person as finger food.

RED BALL CHILLIES STUFFED WITH EMU

Serves 6

600 g emu mince	1/4 bunch continental parsley, finely chopped
1/4 bunch mint, finely chopped	salt and pepper
18 red ball chillies	vegetable oil
2 chillies, de-seeded and finely chopped	600 ml Pandana Leaf Sauce (see recipe page 161)
2 egg yolks	2 bunches baby bok choy

Place the emu, mint, chillies, egg yolks, parsley and salt and pepper in a bowl and combine well. Cut the tops off the red ball chillies and hollow out the inside, removing all the seeds. Stuff the chillies with the emu mixture. Replace the tops of the chillies using toothpicks to secure them.

Fry the chillies in hot vegetable oil for about 3 minutes. Heat the Pandanas Leaf Sauce.

Trim and wash the baby bok choy, blanch it in boiling water for 2–3 minutes and place on the serving plates. Pour some of the sauce over the vegetables and place the chillies on top.

WARM DUCK SALAD WITH BUNYA NUTS AND VINAIGRETTE

Serves 6–8

4 duck breasts
(available from game shops)
1 tablespoon Garlic and Ginger Oil
(see recipe page 158)
1 cup bunya nuts, coarsely sliced
lengthwise
2 medium Spanish onions, cut into
wedge-shaped eighths
2 leeks, finely chopped
1 punnet straw mushrooms, trimmed
1 teaspoon pink peppercorns
1 bunch baby endive, washed, dried and trimmed
salt and pepper, to taste

RED WINE VINAIGRETTE:
1/2 cup balsamic vinegar
1 cup red wine
6 peppercorns
1 bay leaf
1 teaspoon native thyme
1 clove garlic, bruised
1/2 cup olive oil
1 egg yolk

To cook the duck breasts, score the skin with three diagonal cuts. Pan fry with the skin side down for 5 minutes until the duck fat melts away. Turn and cook on the other side for 5 minutes until just cooked. Set aside to cool. Remove the skin and shred the meat.

TO MAKE THE VINAIGRETTE, place the vinegar, wine, peppercorns, bay leaf, thyme and garlic in a saucepan, bring to the boil and reduce by half. Strain, add olive oil then whisk in egg yolk. Remove from the heat and keep warm.

TO MAKE THE DUCK SALAD, place the Garlic and Ginger Oil in a large frying pan and heat until just fragrant. Add the bunya nuts and fry over medium heat until golden brown, then add the onions and leeks and stir fry until just cooked through. Add the mushrooms, peppercorns and duck meat, and heat through. Remove from heat, toss through the endive, season and pour vinaigrette over.

GUM-LEAF-SMOKED WALLABY CARPACCIO WITH BEAN SALAD AND MUNTHARI DRESSING

When Edna ran the canteen at the White Bay Power Station she met an Englishman, Gerry Cadogan, who frequently visited us in Pyrmont. He had two soldier-settler brothers, Pat and Leo, who ran a farm called The Whip near Moss Vale. Before long we were visiting them regularly, and that's where I first tasted the meats of Australia—kangaroo and wallaby, wood ducks, bronze wing pigeons, bush turkeys, even eel and snake.

It was here that I fell in love with the bush. This early love became a passion when I spent nine months on a remote mission station in the Kimberleys. In the Kimberleys I tasted the magnificent native Australian fruits and berries for the first time: bloodnuts, tiny sweet figs and my favourite bush tomatoes.

Serves 6

2 cups borlotti beans
1 cup brown sugar
1 cup rice
4 handfuls gum leaves
3 x 200 g fillets of wallaby (kangaroo will do if wallaby is unavailable)
salt and pepper, to taste
2 ripe tomatoes, finely diced
1 Spanish onion, finely diced
1 small red capsicum, finely diced
2 teaspoons fresh mint, roughly chopped
pinch native mint
18 broad beans

MUNTHARI DRESSING:

1/2 cup dry apple cider
1/2 cup cider vinegar
2 shallots, finely chopped
1/2 cup virgin olive oil
2 teaspoons fresh basil, chopped
2 teaspoons fresh coriander, chopped
pinch native mint
1/4 cup munthari berries
salt and pepper, to taste

To make the dressing, combine all of the ingredients in a blender and blend well. Remove from the blender and reserve.

Soak the borlotti beans in plenty of clean water for 1 hour, drain and rinse, then boil for about 20 minutes or until cooked.

While the beans are cooking, line a baking dish with aluminium foil, and scatter the brown sugar and rice across the bottom. Cover the sugar and rice with the gum leaves, place a cake or baking rack over the leaves, then seal the baking dish with an airtight layer of foil. Set the dish over a flame or on a hotplate at medium to high heat and cook for 8–10 minutes or until the gum leaves are smoking steadily.

Once leaves are smoking well, season the wallaby fillets with salt and pepper then

ON BALGO MISSION STATION

place them on the rack, reseal the foil tightly and bake at 180°C for about 8 minutes. Remove from the oven, take off the foil and allow the fillets to cool. Once cool, wrap each fillet in clingwrap and place in the freezer for 20 minutes. Remove from the freezer and cut into wafer thin slices, carpaccio style.

Place the tomatoes, onion and capsicum in a bowl with the fresh mint, native mint and the cooked borlotti beans. Mix the dressing through gently.

Blanch the broad beans in a pot of boiling water, then refresh under cool water and set aside.

Arrange the wallaby slices and the broad beans around a little mound of dressed bean salad on each plate.

ASPARAGUS TEMPURA WITH BEAN QUANDONG ORANGE CHILLI SALAD

Serves 6

2 bundles asparagus spears
vegetable oil, for frying
1 bunch snake beans, cut into
   3 cm lengths
1 cup quandongs
2 tablespoons coconut shavings
DRESSING:
1 brown onion, peeled and sliced
garlic and ginger oil (see recipe page 158)
1 tablespoon curry powder
2 cups water
1 tablespoon vegetable oil
1 chilli, finely chopped

SALAD:
1 medium Spanish onion, finely sliced
1 tablespoon vegetable oil
1 cup white wine
2 tablespoons pepperleaf
1/2 cup coconut cream
1 tablespoon soy sauce
1 tablespoon coriander, finely chopped
salt and pepper
TEMPURA BATTER:
1 cup self-raising flour
1 pinch turmeric
1 cup ice water

Blanch the asparagus in boiling water and pat dry. Set aside.

To MAKE THE SALAD, blanch the beans in boiling water. Sauté the quandongs in the oil. Set aside until cool, then mix all the salad ingredients together in a bowl.

To MAKE THE DRESSING, sauté the onion and the curry powder together in the vegetable oil until the onion is golden brown. Add the water and white wine and boil until reduced by half. Add the coconut cream, soy sauce, coriander and season.

To MAKE THE TEMPURA BATTER, mix together the flour and turmeric. Add the ice water and mix to a smooth batter. Season with salt and pepper. Refrigerate until needed.

Dip the asparagus in the batter and fry in hot oil. Dress the salad and serve.

WILD GOOSE AND PEPPERBERRY TARTS

This is one of my favourite recipes. We lived briefly in Tasmania, where we looked after a restaurant in Ross; Ray did the food, and I looked after the guests. On our day off we often went to Cradle Mountain. We'd just come back from Balgo and were in love with the bush. There would have been pepperberries in lots of places we visited—mountain pepperberries. In fact, there would have been an amazing array of indigenous food there but we didn't even think of using it. If only we had. Tasmania is a conservative state. They have such rich land and have always had top quality produce, and are now discovering many varieties of native foods.

Makes 6

1 size 18 magpie goose or
1 size 18 goose or duck
MAGPIE GOOSE MARINADE:
4 cloves garlic
1 x 4 cm piece ginger
1/2 cup honey
1/2 cup thick soy sauce
1/2 cup vegetable oil
4 star anise
1 small red chilli, de-seeded

PEPPERBERRY TART PASTRY:
250 g plain flour
100 g cold butter, cut into small cubes
2 tablespoons chopped parsley
1 teaspoon salt
cold water
PEPPERBERRY TART FILLING:
4 shiitake mushrooms, finely sliced
1 green radish, finely sliced
1 tablespoon pepperberries
2 eggs, lightly beaten
1/4 punnet bean sprouts

TO MAKE THE MARINADE, combine all of the ingredients in a blender until smooth, pour over the uncooked goose, and bake the goose at 200°C for about 45 minutes or until cooked through, basting every 10 minutes. When cooked, remove from the oven and set aside to cool, then remove all of the flesh from the bird and slice finely.

TO MAKE THE PASTRY, rub the flour and butter together in a bowl with the fingertips until well combined and the consistency of breadcrumbs. Add the parsley and salt and then the cold water, a little at a time, until the mixture binds together into a firm dough. Wrap the dough in clingwrap and rest in the refrigerator for 30 minutes, then remove and roll out to 3–5 mm thickness. Press rounds of pastry into six 8 cm tart cases. Bake at 150°C for about 15 minutes or until golden brown. Set aside.

TO MAKE THE FILLING, gently combine all of the ingredients with the sliced meat then divide the mixture evenly between the tart cases. Bake the tarts at 180°C for about 8 minutes, or until the egg is firmly set. Serve either hot or cold; if serving hot, accompany the tarts with Pepperberry Jus (see recipe on page 172).

POACHED FISH DUMPLINGS WITH LIME OIL SALSA

My father Abe made gefilte fish long before I was born and certainly until the day he died. It was his favourite of all favourite dishes.

Makes about 20 dumplings

3 cloves garlic, finely chopped

1 x 2.5 cm knob ginger, finely chopped

2 leeks, finely chopped

1 brown onion, finely chopped

vegetable oil

1 kg minced white fish
  (e.g. flathead or snapper)

1 cup chopped bunya nuts

1/2 bunch Thai basil, stems removed and
  reserved, leaves finely chopped

1/4 cup coconut cream

1 egg, lightly beaten

1 cup breadcrumbs

2 chillies, de-seeded and finely chopped

zest and juice of 1 lime

salt and pepper, to taste

SALSA:

1 small red capsicum, finely chopped

1 small yellow capsicum, finely chopped

1 medium Spanish onion, finely chopped

10 bush cucumbers

1 green chilli, de-seeded and finely chopped

1 bunch fresh coriander, finely chopped (don't use stems)

juice and zest of 1 lime

1 cup olive oil

100 ml white wine vinegar

2 teaspoons lime oil (this can be purchased from
  specialty food shops)

TO MAKE THE SALSA, combine the red and yellow capsicums, onion and cucumber in a bowl, then mix through the chilli and coriander. Add the lime juice and zest, olive oil, white wine vinegar and lime oil, mix thoroughly and set aside.

TO MAKE THE DUMPLINGS, fry the garlic, ginger, leeks and onions in the oil until golden brown. Remove from the heat and set aside to cool, then combine well with the minced fish, bunya nuts, Thai basil, coconut cream, egg, breadcrumbs, chilli, lime juice and zest and salt and pepper. Shape the mixture into balls about half the size of a golf ball, and poach in a pot of steadily simmering water with the Thai basil stems. When the dumplings bob to the surface and appear slightly fluffy, cook for a further 3 minutes. Remove from the water with a slotted spoon.

Serve the dumplings hot or cold with the salsa, garnished with a few sprigs of coriander. For a more substantial dish, add rounds of char-grilled eggplant and some mixed salad leaves. For finger food, serve cold on platters with a sweet chilli dipping sauce.

ANTIPASTO WITH KANGAROO PROSCIUTTO WITH BABY BEETROOT LEAVES AND GUM-LEAF AND PEPPERBERRY OIL

Serves 6

250 ml olive oil

2 large pepperberries

small handful gum leaves

1 large red capsicum

1 large yellow capsicum

100 ml vegetable oil, extra

salt, to taste

2 tablespoons pepperleaf

2 medium eggplants

250 g Timboon fetta cheese (substitute Australian or Greek fetta)

200 g kangaroo prosciutto (sliced very thin)

250 g baby beetroot leaves

Place the oil, pepperberries and gum leaves in a saucepan. Simmer for 1 hour. Strain and set aside.

While the oil is being prepared, rub down the red and yellow capsicums with the extra oil, salt and pepperleaf, then bake at 200°C for 10–15 minutes, turning frequently. When the skins are slightly blistered, remove and set aside to cool, then peel and de-seed. You may find this easier if you place the capsicums in a plastic bag to cool.

Spread the peeled capsicums on a board and, using a round scone cutter, cut out 6 circular pieces from each. Aim for a similar-sized diameter to that of the eggplants.

Slice the eggplants crosswise into 1 cm thick rounds, rub the flesh on each side with the oil, salt and pepperleaf, and char grill or grill on high heat for 3–4 minutes per side or until browned and cooked through.

Cut the fetta cheese into round, 1 cm thick slices. Place the kangaroo prosciutto and beetroot leaf in a bowl with the gum leaf and pepperberry oil and toss until well coated.

Assemble the antipasto on individual plates by layering a round of eggplant, then red capsicum, fetta cheese and another eggplant, and top with yellow capsicum. Arrange the prosciutto and beetroot leaves around each timbale, and serve.

CROCODILE SWAG BAGS

When Ray and I went up to see the Sepik River in Papua New Guinea, we were completely overawed by the sheer number of crocodiles there. This is a very wide river and after the monsoon rains huge chunks of land would tear away from the banks and remain in the swollen river. It was weird to be out there at night time, floating around these miniature islands. In the dark you could make out hundreds of sparkling little lights—each one the beady eye of a crocodile assessing our nutritional value. It was a frightening sight.

The wife of the captain of the houseboat we were travelling on came from Papua New Guinea. She'd cooked some crocodile and we ate it cold with our buffet lunch. As we were eating we heard the news over the radio of the croc fatalities for the day—not road fatalities, but croc fatalities—but it didn't turn us off eating this delicious tender meat.

2 leeks, sliced into 1/2 cm strips (reserving several whole sheets of outer leek leaves)	1 large carrot, sliced into julienne strips 3 cm x 2 mm x 2 mm
4 tablespoons Garlic and Ginger Oil (see recipe page 158)	2 medium zucchinis, sliced into julienne strips 3 cm x 2 mm x 2 mm
500 g minced crocodile meat	salt and pepper, to taste
1 large corn cob, kernels cut off	16 sheets rice paper 8–10 cm rectangular
	vegetable oil

Sauté the leeks in the Garlic and Ginger Oil until soft, then set aside to cool.

Combine the crocodile meat, corn kernels, carrot and zucchinis with the sliced leeks and season with salt and pepper.

Cut the reserved leek leaves lengthwise to form 16 ribbons 15–20 cm long and 5 mm wide and blanch in boiling water for 1–2 minutes.

Blanch the rice paper in boiling water for a few seconds until pliable. Place 2 tablespoons (or 1 tablespoon if the swag bags are to be used as finger food) of the crocodile mixture into the centre of each rectangle, then gather the edges of the rice paper above the mixture and tie securely with the leek ribbons. Deep fry the swag bags in oil for about 3 minutes or until crisp and golden, then drain well on kitchen paper.

Serve on mixed salad leaves with Native Mint Pesto (see recipe page 167) or with a sweet chilli dipping sauce.

Makes 16 swag bags (2 each as a starter, or 1 each for finger food).

CROCODILE SWAG BAGS

WESTERN AUSTRALIAN SEARED SCALLOPS WITH NATIVE ANISEED AND SAFFRON JUS

1/2 fennel bulb, sliced into
   5 cm x 2 mm x 2 mm lengths
1 Chinese radish, sliced into
   5 cm x 2 mm x 2 mm lengths
1 leek, sliced into
   5 cm x 2 mm x 2 mm lengths
4 tablespoons Garlic and Ginger Oil
   (see recipe page 158)

18 Western Australian scallops, in the shell
NATIVE ANISEED AND SAFFRON JUS:
1 litre fish stock
1/2 teaspoon native aniseed
1 pinch saffron
juice and zest of 1 lime
salt and pepper, to taste

To make the jus, combine all of the ingredients in a saucepan and simmer over low heat until the liquid has reduced by half. Season with salt and pepper.

Meanwhile, stir fry the fennel, radish and leek in the Garlic and Ginger Oil for 3 minutes or until barely softened.

Remove the scallops from their shells, clean the shells, and spread them onto a tray or bench. Divide the sautéed vegetable mixture evenly among the shells, making a little bed of vegetable on each shell.

Sear the scallops in a very hot frying pan brushed with a little oil for 1–2 minutes or until just cooked through. Place the scallops on top of the vegetables in the shells, drizzle with the warm jus and serve.

Serves 6 as a starter, or allow 1 per person for finger food.

TWICE COOKED CRISPY DUCK WITH CHINESE BROCCOLI AND DAVIDSON PLUM SAUCE PG 104

SALAD OF MAGPIE GOOSE WRAPPED IN CHINESE CABBAGE WITH CRISPY NOODLES AND QUANDONG SAUCE

Serves 6

1 magpie goose or size 18 duck

olive oil

Chinese wet noodles (available
   from Asian grocery stores)

QUANDONG SAUCE:

250 g quandongs, roughly chopped

1 x 2.5 cm knob ginger, finely chopped

1/2 bunch coriander, roots and leaves
   separated, chopped

1 clove garlic, roughly chopped

500 ml goose or chicken stock

juice of 1 lime

1/2 cup honey

2 small red chillies, de-seeded and
   finely chopped

1/2 Spanish onion, finely chopped

GOOSE SALAD:

1 medium green radish

3 leeks

3 carrots

2 cloves garlic, finely chopped

1 x 3 cm knob ginger, finely chopped

2–3 small red chillies, de-seeded and finely chopped

2 tablespoons fish sauce

juice of 2 limes

salt and pepper, to taste

vegetable oil

1 Chinese cabbage

Roast the goose at 180°C for about 45 minutes. Remove from the oven and cool, then shred the flesh into very fine strips about 5 cm long and 2 mm wide and thick. This can be done well ahead.

TO MAKE THE QUANDONG SAUCE, combine the quandongs, ginger, coriander roots and garlic with the stock in a saucepan over low heat, then add the lime juice and honey. Bring to the boil, then remove from the heat and purée. Add the coriander leaves, chillies and onion and stir well.

TO MAKE THE SALAD, slice the radish, leeks and carrots into similar-sized pieces using a mandolin slicer or a very sharp knife and a patient approach.

Heat the oil in a large, heavy-based frying pan and sauté the garlic, ginger and chillies for 1–2 minutes or until fragrant. Add the sliced vegetables and sauté for a further 1–2 minutes, then add the fish sauce and lime juice and continue to sauté until the vegetables are cooked through but still fairly crunchy. Remove from the heat and cool. Add the shredded goose meat, toss until well combined. Season with salt and pepper. This can also be prepared ahead of time.

TO MAKE THE CABBAGE ROLLS, carefully remove the large outer leaves from the cabbage (you will need 12 leaves) and blanch in boiling water for 1 minute, then refresh in cold water. Pat the leaves dry with kitchen paper and trim off any hard stem, taking care to keep each leaf in one piece. Lay the blanched leaves flat in pairs, overlapping them so that they form rectangular sheets about 10 cm x 20 cm. Press firmly at the overlap points so they stick together.

Place a portion of goose meat mixture in a sausage-shaped mound in the middle of each cabbage mat. Fold the top and bottom ends over the goose meat, and roll the cabbage up tightly around the meat like a big spring roll.

Form the noodles into individual nests about half the size of your fist and deep fry at 180°C, turning occasionally, until golden. Drain on kitchen paper.

Slice each cabbage roll into 3 portions and serve cold on a nest of noodles in a pool of quandong sauce. Garnish with a sprig of coriander.

BABY OCTOPUS WITH NATIVE PEPPERLEAF AND SQUID INK PASTA

It was in Terrigal that we first met a remarkable American—Woody the chef. He was a great spear-fisherman and often brought his catch in for the customers at the Hotel Florida. He told us that the best way to tenderise abalone was to throw it in the washing machine! (Don't use washing powder!)

Serves 6

1 kg baby octopus, cleaned, beaks removed	500 g squid ink pasta
2 cups vegetable oil	pinch salt
8 whole garlic cloves, peeled	1 tablespoon native pepperleaf

Place the octopus in a heat-proof container. Bring the oil and garlic cloves to the boil in a saucepan over low heat, let boil for 1–2 minutes then remove from the heat and pour over the cleaned octopus, which should be submerged. Leave to cool.

Cook the pasta in a large pot of boiling salted water until al dente (that is, tender but still firm). Drain.

Remove the octopus from the oil and place it on a very hot char-grill or barbecue or in a frying pan. Sprinkle with the salt and native pepperleaf, leaving a little in reserve, and cook, turning frequently, for 2–3 minutes.

Place the cooked pasta and octopus in a large frying pan, add a splash of the garlic oil and the remaining salt and native pepperleaf and toss over high heat for 1–2 minutes or until warmed through. Serve immediately.

ZUCCHINI FLOWERS STUFFED WITH QUEENSLAND MUD CRAB, KUMERA, CORN AND NATIVE MINT

Raymond came to visit me in New Guinea and we travelled to the top of the Sepik River by boat, then flew back to Port Moresby. The scenes that we saw along the way, the exotic costumes, the dancing and the feeling of celebration was extraordinary. Even finishing a string bag could be an occasion for a sing-sing. Sometimes there would be three days of dancing and singing. We loved their sense of theatre, and their extraordinary costumes—stunning plumes, leaves and fabrics. Raymond said there were more feathers than the Ziegfield Follies.

This was in 1978, so not many people visited this remote region. That's when Ray saw pumpkin flowers being used as a vegetable. These are just a bit bigger than zucchini flowers. When he came back to Port Moresby he used the flowers for the first time. He stuffed them with seafood and corn, both abundant in Port Moresby.

400 g kumera	1 corn cob, kernels sliced from it
1 tablespoon garlic, finely chopped	500 g crab meat
1 tablespoon ginger, finely chopped	1 egg, lightly beaten
2 leeks, finely sliced	salt and pepper, to taste
4 tablespoons olive oil	16 zucchini flowers
2 tablespoons chopped mint	Light Batter (see recipe page 168)
1 teaspoon native mint	olive oil, extra
2 chillies, de-seeded and chopped	

Boil the kumera for about 7–10 minutes (it only needs to be half-cooked), strain, cool and roughly dice.

Sauté the garlic, ginger and leeks in the oil until barely softened and fragrant, then add the mint, native mint and chillies and continue sautéeing for 2–3 minutes more. Remove from the heat and set aside to cool.

Combine the kumera, sautéed ingredients, corn kernels and crab meat together in a bowl, mix the egg through thoroughly and season with salt and pepper. Place the mixture in a piping bag and stuff each zucchini flower with the mixture.

Coat each flower with Light Batter (alternatively, the flowers can be lightly dusted with flour, coated with beaten egg and covered in breadcrumbs). Fry in about 1 cm of oil until golden.

Serve with mixed lettuce leaves, or as finger food with a dipping sauce of mayonnaise to which a little lemon juice or lemon myrtle has been added (see recipes for Lemon Myrtle Dressing or Lemon Aspen Mayonnaise on page 159).

Serves 8 as a starter, or allow 1 per person as finger food.

MUSHROOMS STUFFED WITH EMU AND BLACK RICE

Ray and I visited Bali and were struck by the way they used black rice. They use it as a sweet with palm sugar, chopped up fresh fruit and grated fresh coconut. Raymond has been known to have two or three bowls of this before he starts the day. However, we were using black rice in the early 1980's, much to the astonishment of our customers who were convinced we'd dyed it black.

It stands up to cooking, has an interesting chewy texture and goes with so many things.

Serves 6

1 1/2 cups uncooked black rice

6 large or 12 medium cupped mushrooms

4 bacon rashers, roughly diced

4 tablespoons Garlic and Ginger Oil
(see recipe page 158)

1 leek, finely sliced

1 stick celery, finely sliced

salt and pepper, to taste

500 g minced emu meat

1/4 cup sesame seeds

1 3/4 cups breadcrumbs, for crumbing

2 eggs

1/2 cup milk

1/2 cup plain flour

Cook the rice in boiling salted water for 20-25 minutes or until sticky. Drain and set aside.

Remove the stalks of the mushrooms, and hollow out the mushroom cups to form a shell. Roughly dice the leftover stalks and flesh and retain.

Fry the bacon in the Garlic and Ginger Oil for 2–3 minutes. Add the leek and celery, cook for a further 2–3 minutes, then add the leftover mushroom flesh and stalks and salt and pepper. When they are partly cooked, remove from the heat and set aside to cool. When cool, add the emu meat and the rice and combine well. Fill the mushrooms with the mixture, pressing it firmly into each mushroom cup.

Combine the sesame seeds and breadcrumbs, and pour onto a flat plate. Beat together the eggs and milk, and lay the flour out on a plate. Roll each mushroom in the flour, then the egg and milk mixture, then in the breadcrumbs until well coated.

Bake the mushrooms, flat side up, at 180°C in a shallow pan brushed with a little oil for about 15 minutes or until golden.

To serve, place the mushrooms on serving plates and garnish with mixed salad leaves and a dressing such as Black Bean Dressing (see recipe page 160).

PEPPERBERRY–SEARED BUFFALO SALAD WITH BLACK BEAN DRESSING

In Wyndham we stayed at the presbytery of the Catholic Church. The priest there was an unusual Jesuit, rather hippy, who played the guitar eight hours a day. Slim Dusty came to town and this priest said we should go and see him perform. We had hardly heard of Slim Dusty—we just knew he was some remote country and western singer.

We went down to the pub and, for the first time, had buffalo for dinner. The place was full of mining characters who had lobbed into town; they were all going off to this Slim Dusty concert—an open air concert. The Aborigines loved 'Slum' Dusty and all of them could sing his songs for six, seven, eight hours a day without stopping. The elders still sang traditional songs, but the young ones went for 'Slum' Dusty. Slim was a god all across the northern top of Australia.

That concert was one of the greatest concerts I've ever been to. The rhythm of the Aboriginal people, their bodies swaying to his music, the starry night and the music. It was one of the great nights of my life.

Serves 6-8

600 g buffalo fillet

100 g sea salt

3 tablespoons ground pepperberry

100 ml vegetable oil

500 ml Black Bean Dressing
(see recipe page 160)

1 zucchini, sliced into strips 5 cm x 2 mm x 2 mm

1 cucumber, sliced into strips 5 cm x 2 mm x 2 mm

1 carrot, sliced into strips 5 cm x 2 mm x 2 mm

chervil

Oven-dried Romano Tomatoes (see page 160), optional

Trim all visible fat and sinew from the buffalo. Combine the salt and ground pepperberry and rub the meat down with this mixture until it is well coated.

Coat a heavy-based baking tray with the oil, and place over high heat until the oil is smoking. Sear the buffalo in the hot oil, browning it on all sides, then bake at 220°C for 5 minutes (longer if you prefer well-cooked meat). Remove from the oven and set aside to cool.

Toss the Black Bean Dressing through the combined zucchini, cucumber and carrot and place the mixture in little piles on each plate. Slice the buffalo very thinly, then fan the meat slices over the salad. Drizzle with a little more dressing, and garnish with a piece of chervil. Add some oven-dried Romano tomatoes for extra interest and flavour.

TRAVELLING IN OUTBACK AUSTRALIA

ATLANTIC SALMON GRAVLAX WITH LEMON MYRTLE AND WATTLE SEED BLINI

Serves 6–8

400g Atlantic salmon fillets, skin on	**WATTLE SEED BLINIS:**
150 g sugar	1 tablespoon wattle seeds
150 g rock salt	3 eggs
4 tablespoons seeded Dijon mustard	2/3 cup milk
3 tablespoons lemon myrtle	2/3 cup water
1/2 cup Lemon Myrtle Dressing	1/3 cup canola oil
(see recipe page 159)	2 cups self-raising flour
lamb's tongue lettuce leaves, washed	2 teaspoons caster sugar
and dried	

Wash the salmon fillets, pat them dry, then sprinkle the skinless side with a thick coating of sugar, pressing firmly into the flesh. Repeat this procedure with the rock salt, forming a layer over the sugar. Wrap the salmon tightly in clingwrap, and stand in the refrigerator for 24 hours.

Brush the salt and sugar from the salmon fillets, rinse them under fresh water and pat dry. Spread the skinless side with a layer of mustard, then sprinkle a layer of lemon myrtle over this.

TO MAKE THE BLINIS, fry the wattle seeds in a frying pan over low heat for 2–3 minutes to enhance the flavour.

Whisk together the eggs, milk, water and oil until well combined. Gradually add the flour, wattle seeds and sugar, stirring well to form a pancake-like batter. If the batter seems too thick, add a little extra water or milk. Rest the mixture in the refrigerator for 30 minutes.

Pour a scant tablespoon of the mixture into egg rings in a well-greased frying pan and cook as you would pancakes.

Slice the salmon very thinly, severing each slice from the skin. Brush one side of each blini with a little Lemon Myrtle Dressing (alternatively, you can use a well-whisked vinaigrette made with plenty of Dijon mustard and lemon juice), then arrange 2 blinis per serving plate alongside a little pile of lamb's tongue lettuce, dressed side up. Spread 2 or 3 slices of salmon on each blini, sprinkle with a little more dressing and serve. For finger food, simply spread each blini with dressing and top with lamb's tongue lettuce and salmon.

EGGPLANT STUFFED WITH PRAWNS, CUTTLEFISH AND NATIVE ANISEED

Serves 4–6

400 g cuttlefish (or squid), minced in a food processor

400 g peeled prawns, roughly chopped

1 capsicum, finely chopped

1 leek, finely sliced

1/2 fennel bulb, finely sliced

2 teaspoons native aniseed

4 tablespoons Garlic and Ginger Oil (see recipe page 158)

2 tablespoons fresh basil, finely chopped

salt and pepper, to taste

2 medium eggplants

Combine the cuttlefish and prawns. Sauté the capsicum, leek, fennel and native aniseed in the Garlic and Ginger Oil until well softened and fragrant. Add the seafood, mix well and remove from the heat. Stir through the basil and seasonr.

Cut the eggplants into 2 cm rounds then, using a sharp knife, make a deep cut in the centre of the 'rim' of each round, cutting deep inside the eggplant to form a pocket. Using a piping bag, pipe the mixture into the eggplant pockets, then press the opening at the rim of the wheel closed. Brush each pocket with oil, and cook on a hot char grill or frying pan for 7 minutes on each side or until well cooked.

Serve with crisp salad greens.

SALMON TARTARE

Serves 4–6

800 g fresh Atlantic salmon (skinned and deboned), finely chopped

2 medium chillies, finely chopped

1/2 bunch coriander, finely chopped

1 knob ginger, finely chopped

6 caper berries, finely chopped

100 g fennel bulb, finely chopped

15 g fennel leaf, finely chopped

2 egg yolks

1 teaspoon sesame oil

1 teaspoon native aniseed

1 teaspoon fish sauce

1 small Spanish onion, peeled and finely chopped

2 limes, juice and zest

To Serve:

fresh noodles

tetsoi leaves, blanched

crème fraîche

ocean trout roe

Mix the ingredients together in a bowl excluding those for serving. Deep fry small handfuls of noodles to make nests. To serve place tetsoi leaves on the plates then a noodle bundle, top with salmon mix and a scant teaspoon of crème fraîche and garnish with ocean trout roe.

WHITING FILLETS WITH BAKED EGGPLANT AND BUSH CUCUMBER SALAD WITH NATIVE ANISEED DRESSING

Serves 6

2–3 very small whiting or similar fish fillets per person

BUSH CUCUMBER SALAD:

1 eggplant

24 bush cucumbers

1 fennel bulb, thinly sliced

1 Spanish onion, thinly sliced

1 tablespoon pink Japanese pickled ginger

1 tablespoon fresh basil leaves, chopped

zest of 1 lime

DRESSING:

100 g sugar

100 ml water

1 teaspoon native aniseed

100 ml vegetable oil

1 1/2 teaspoons chilli, finely chopped

2 cloves garlic, finely chopped

60 ml soy sauce

100 ml cider vinegar

juice of 1 lime

TO MAKE THE DRESSING, place the sugar and water in a saucepan and bring to the boil, then add all remaining ingredients. Simmer for 5 minutes until reduced, then remove from heat and set aside to cool.

TO MAKE THE SALAD, bake the eggplant whole on a lightly oiled tray at 150°C for about 20 minutes, or until partly cooked i.e. soft, but still holding its shape. Remove from the oven and, when cooled, cut into 6 x 2 cm uniformly sized rounds. Roughly dice any eggplant portions that are too small plus the end pieces, and combine with the bush cucumber, fennel bulb, onion, ginger, basil and lime zest. Toss the dressing through the salad.

Just before serving, pan fry the whiting fillets in butter for 1–2 minutes per side, or batter them and deep fry for 3 minutes, whichever is preferred, taking care not to overcook the fillets or they will fall apart.

To serve, place an eggplant round on each plate and pile the salad over. Arrange the hot whiting fillets on top of the salad and serve immediately.

OCEAN TROUT WITH SAUTEED ASIAN SALAD

Serves 6

3/4 cup white wine

1 clove bruised garlic

1/2 onion, finely chopped

10 peppercorns

1 bayleaf

2 cups fish stock

12 oyster mushrooms, sliced into thirds

1 large bunch bok choy

200 g Oven-dried Romano Tomatoes (see recipe page 160)

2 tablespoons pepperleaf

2 tablespoons mustard seeds

1 eggplant

6 x 800 g fillets ocean trout

200 g cold butter, cubed

salt, extra and pepper, to taste

Place the wine in a saucepan with the garlic, onion, peppercorns and bayleaf. Bring to a slow simmer and cook until reduced by half. Add the fish stock and simmer until reduced again by one-third. Turn off the heat and strain. While the wine and stock is reducing, combine the mushrooms, bok choy, tomatoes, pepperleaf and mustard seeds in a bowl.

Slice the eggplants crosswise into rounds 2–3 cm thick and fry in a little butter until soft, or deep fry in oil until golden brown. Drain off the excess oil, and keep on the bottom shelf of the oven on low heat to keep warm.

The fish can be cooked in one of three ways: pan fry in oil and butter for 3–4 minutes per side, taking care not to overcook; or, brush each fillet with oil and char grill for 3–4 minutes per side; or, seal the fillets in a hot frying pan and bake, covered with foil, at 200°C for 6–8 minutes or until cooked through.

While the fish is cooking, return the wine and stock to high heat. When boiling remove from the heat and whisk in the butter, a few cubes at a time, until it is well combined. Don't reboil. Season with salt and pepper.

Sauté the mushrooms, bok choy, tomatoes, mustard seeds and pepperleaf for 2–3 minutes in a little butter until just softened and heated through.

To serve, place the warm eggplant on a serving plate and top with the fish fillets. Set the sautéed vegetables on top of the fillets, then drizzle with the wine and stock sauce.

FILLET OF CURED SALMON WITH CRISPY NOODLES AND LEMON MYRTLE AND SUN-DRIED TOMATO DRESSING

Curing the salmon in this mixture infuses it with the flavours of lime and dill, and it is as simple as marinading the fillets in the refrigerator for 24 hours.

Serves 6–8

6 x 200g Atlantic salmon fillets

250 g wet Chinese noodles

vegetable oil

18-24 lettuce or rocket leaves

**fresh or deep-fried lemon
    myrtle leaves, optional**

CURING MIXTURE:

2 cups sugar

1 cup rock salt

1/2 bunch dill

zest and juice of 2 limes

3 lemon myrtle leaves

2 tablespoons cracked pepper

LEMON MYRTLE AND SUN-DRIED TOMATO DRESSING:

3 egg yolks

1 tablespoon Dijon mustard

20 ml white wine vinegar

200 ml water

500 ml vegetable oil

4 tablespoons lemon myrtle

2 teaspoons boiling water

3 tablespoons sun-dried tomatoes

salt and pepper, to taste

Prepare the salmon 24 hours in advance. Remove any bones from the fish. Combine all of the curing mixture ingredients and spread half over the base of any shallow, non-metal dish big enough to hold all of the fillets in a single layer (a plastic tray or large ceramic baking dish would be ideal). Spread the remaining half of the mixture on top of the salmon. Cover the dish with clingwrap and place in the refrigerator for 24 hours.

To make the dressing, combine the egg yolks, mustard, vinegar and water in a bowl and whisk until the yolks are thick and pale. Slowly add the oil, a few drops at a time, beating continuously until all of the oil has been used and the mixture has a mayonnaise-like consistency.

Infuse the lemon myrtle in the boiling water—this will enhance its flavour and aroma. Add to the dressing with the sun-dried tomatoes, then purée in a food processor for 2 minutes (this enhances the flavour and colour). Season to taste.

To cook the noodles, twist them into 6–8 nests, each about the size of a golf ball, and deep fry in hot oil for 1–2 minutes or until crisp—be careful not to overcook. Drain the noodle nests on kitchen paper, set aside and keep warm.

Rinse the salmon thoroughly and, if using a whole fish, slice into the desired number of portions with a very sharp knife. Seal on all sides in a hot, lightly oiled pan—cook only until the fish is warmed through, as the curing process makes further cooking unnecessary.

To serve, spread some dressing onto each serving plate and place a few rocket or lettuce leaves in the centre. Top the leaves with the crispy noodles, then the seared salmon.

STIR-FRIED SCAMPI, MUNTHARI BERRIES AND ASIAN GREENS

Serves 6–8

4 onions, finely diced

18 Western Australian scampi, halved lengthwise

SAUCE:

1 litre white wine

500 ml chicken stock

1 litre fish stock

1 pinch saffron

salt and pepper, to taste

ASIAN GREENS:

6 shitake mushrooms, finely sliced

2 punnets straw mushrooms

78 munthari berries

2 bunches choy sum, roughly chopped

vegetable oil

For the sauce, reduce the white wine by half. Add the chicken and fish stock with the saffron. Reduce to one-third.

In a large ovenproof pan, heat some vegetable oil and sauté the onion. Place the halved scampi in the pan with the meat facing up. Pour half the sauce over the scampi and place in an oven at 200°C for 3 minutes or until the scampi are cooked.

In a seperate pan heat some oil and butter and add the Asian mix. Sauté lightly until cooked.

To serve place the greens on the plate, divided between six servings. Divide the scampi evenly between the plates. Ladle the sauce over the scampi.

BAKED BABY BARRAMUNDI WITH CARAMELISED TEMPEH AND BUSH TOMATO SAUCE

In Bali we had a friend who ran a simple place where she cooked for locals and the odd tourist. It was vegetarian with a little bit of fish and game—but mainly vegetarian because she was so poor. Not a glamorous place, but she was an extraordinary cook. That's when we first had tempeh, which is made from soya bean. You slice it and deep fry it or you can also bake it. We loved it and have cooked with it ever since. Its lovely nutty flavour combined with the cooked crispiness makes it a really special dish.

Serves 6

250 g tempeh

1/2 cup brown sugar or palm sugar

1 chilli, de-seeded and finely chopped

1 tablespoon Indonesian soy sauce

2 leeks, finely sliced

1/2 enchoy, leaves separated

4 tablespoons Garlic and Ginger Oil (see recipe page 158)

6 whole baby barramundi, approximately 200 g each, scaled (ask the fishmonger to do this)

1 tablespoon bush tomato

Bush Tomato Sauce (see recipe page 162)

Slice the tempeh very thinly, and pan fry it in a little oil for 1–2 minutes per side or until golden. Drain off any excess oil, and spread on a baking tray.

Caramelise the sugar by melting it over low heat with the chilli, stirring constantly, until golden brown. When it is bubbling gently, remove it from the heat then thoroughly blend in the soy sauce. Drizzle the caramelised sugar over the tempeh and leave it to set for 10–15 minutes.

Sauté the leeks and enchoy in the Garlic and Ginger Oil, remove from the heat and divide into 6 portions. Place one portion inside each barramundi. Brush the fish with a little Garlic and Ginger Oil, then sprinkle with bush tomato. Bake at 180°C for about 15 minutes or until the flesh is springy but not dried out.

Sprinkle the top of each fish with the caramelised tempeh. Serve the barramundi with Bush Tomato Sauce.

BAKED BABY BARRUMUNDI WITH CARAMELISED TEMPEH AND BUSH TOMATO SAUCE

Wrap the silver beet tightly around the sides of each fish, leaving the herbed top exposed to form a sort of 'tray' so the silver beet should keep it clear of the paperbark fibres. Wrap a sheet of paperbark around each spinach parcel in the same way, leaving the herbed top exposed, and tie at each end like a bonbon with kitchen twine. Bake the trout at 180°C for 12–15 minutes or until the herbed top is crusty and aromatic and the flesh of the fish has a nice spring to it.

Serve the fish with crispy stir-fried vegetables, with the aoli on the side.

BAKED BLUE-EYE COD WRAPPED IN PAPERBARK WITH A BUSH TOMATO, LEMON MYRTLE AND MACADAMIA CRUST

Serves 6

6 large silver beet leaves, stalks removed at the base of the leaf
1/2 bunch enchoy
6 sheets paperbark 20 cm square, pre-soaked in water for 10 minutes

6 x 200 g fillets blue-eye cod
6 teaspoons bush tomato
6 teaspoons lemon myrtle
6 tablespoons macadamia nuts, roughly chopped

Blanch the silver beet leaves and the enchoy in boiling water, then plunge in iced water. Pat dry, taking care to leave the silver beet leaves whole. Set aside.

Lay out the paperbark, and spread a silver beet leaf over the centre of each bark piece—this forms a layer that will protect the fish from the fibres in the bark. Divide the enchoy into 6 portions, and place each portion in the centre of each silver beet piece. Position the fish fillets over the enchoy. Sprinkle one half of the exposed top of the fillet with the bush tomato and the other half with the lemon myrtle, then spread a band of chopped macadamias down the centre. Bring the edges of the paperbark up around each fish fillet and tie tightly at the top side with kitchen twine so the fish is exposed. Place on a lightly oiled baking tray and bake at 180°C for about 20 minutes or until cooked through.

Lift the fish away from the paperbark, and serve with a rocket salad.

NATIVE FETTUCCINE WITH STUFFED PRAWNS AND LEMON MYRTLE PRAWN BISQUE

Serves 6

12 green king prawns

1/2 bunch mint, finely chopped

1/4 bunch continental parsley, finely chopped

2 chillies, finely chopped

200 g royal red prawns, peeled and
   heads removed

400 g redfish fillets, skinned and boned

12 silver beet leaves

salt and pepper, to taste

1 kg native fettuccine (available from
   specialist suppliers)

mint or coriander leaves, to garnish

LEMON MYRTLE PRAWN BISQUE:

4 cloves garlic, roughly chopped

1 x 4 cm knob ginger, roughly chopped

1 chilli, roughly chopped

1 onion, roughly chopped

1 leek, roughly chopped

1 carrot, roughly chopped

1 stick celery, roughly chopped

2 tablespoons lemon myrtle

150 g butter

3 kg prawn heads and shells

6 lemon myrtle leaves

3 tablespoons tomato paste

3 litres water

350 ml tomato juice

salt and pepper, to taste

1 lime juiced

To make the bisque, sauté the garlic, ginger, chilli, onion, leek, carrot, celery and lemon myrtle in the butter for about 5 minutes or until softened and fragrant. Add the prawn shells and heads, lemon myrtle leaves and tomato paste and sauté for a further 5 minutes. Add the water and tomato juice, bring to the boil, then reduce the heat and simmer for 1 hour. Remove from the heat and purée the mixture including the heads and shells. Strain well, then return to the saucepan and cook over low heat until reduced by about half. Season to taste.

Remove the shells of the king prawns, retaining the heads and tails. Slice the body of the prawns along the back almost all the way through. Remove the vein and flatten the prawns out (you may need to make a couple of nicks just below the base of the head to do this easily) then set aside in the refrigerator.

In a food processor, blend the mint, parsley, chillies, school prawns and redfish fillets to a paste. Spread each king prawn with a thick layer of the paste, then return to the refrigerator.

Blanch the silver beet leaves in boiling water, then plunge in iced water. Pat dry with kitchen paper, taking care to keep the leaves whole and untorn. Slice off the white stem at the base of the leaf. Wrap each prawn tightly in a silver beet leaf. If the prawns are being made ahead of time, they can be prepared to this stage and stored in the refrigerator for 24 hours.

Just before serving brush the prawn parcels thoroughly with vegetable oil and arrange on a well-oiled baking tray. Bake at 180°C for 15 minutes, turning occasionally. While the prawns are in the oven, cook the fettuccine in boiling salted water until al dente. Drain.

To serve, arrange the prawn parcels on top of the pasta and cover with the bisque. Garnish with a few mint or coriander leaves.

POACHED ATLANTIC SALMON IN PAPERBARK WITH WARRIGAL GREENS AND LEMON MYRTLE

Serves 6

6 large silver beet leaves

3 cups warrigal greens

6 x 200 g Atlantic salmon fillets

zest of 12 lemons

water or fish stock

5 fresh lemon myrtle leaves

3 fresh leaves pepperleaf

salt

6 sheets paperbark 20 cm square, pre-soaked in water for 10 minutes

Blanch the silver beet leaves and warrigal greens in boiling water, then plunge in iced water. Pat dry. Remove the white stalks of the silver beet at the base of the leaf, and lay them out flat.

Place a small pile of warrigal greens on the centre of each silver beet leaf, then top with a salmon fillet. Sprinkle the salmon with a little lemon zest, then wrap the silver beet leaf tightly around the fish. Fold the paperbark tightly around the silver beet and salmon parcel and tie up, giftwrap style.

Fill a fish kettle or large saucepan with the water or fish stock and add the lemon myrtle, pepperleaf and salt. Bring to the boil, then reduce the heat to a gentle simmer. Add the salmon parcels to the water and poach for 10–12 minutes. Remove from the poaching water and drain on a teatowel.

Serve with a salad of mixed leaves and a sauce or dressing such as Watercress and Pepperleaf Oil (see recipe page 158).

POU

CHICKEN BREAST WITH BUSH TOMATO CRUST AND CHILLI RATATOUILLE

Serves 6

8 tablespoons bush tomato

25 ml olive oil

6 corn-fed chicken breasts

CHILLI RATATOUILLE:

1 large red capsicum

1 large yellow capsicum

salt and pepper, to taste

1 large eggplant, cut into batons
  1 cm x 1 cm x 5 cm

salt

1 large zucchini, cut into batons
  1 cm x 1 cm x 5 cm

2 medium Spanish onions, cut in half and then
  into 2–3 cm slices

2 tablespoons Garlic and Ginger Oil (see recipe page 158)

2 chillies, de-seeded and finely chopped

To make the ratatouille, season the capsicums with salt and pepper and place on a baking tray. Bake at 180°C for about 20 minutes or until the skin is soft and well wrinkled. Place them in a bowl, seal tightly with clingwrap and refrigerate for 10–15 minutes, or until they are partly cooled (this will make them easier to peel). When the capsicums are cooled and peeled, remove the seeds and cut them into pieces about the same size as the eggplant and zucchini.

Combine the bush tomato and oil, and rub into the chicken breasts. Sear the coated breasts for 1–2 minutes per side, then bake at 200°C for 10–15 minutes or until cooked. Slice the chicken breasts into 4 to 5 pieces each.

While the chicken is in the oven, continue making the ratatouille by sautéing the zucchini, eggplant and onions in the Garlic and Ginger Oil until soft but not soggy. Add the chillies and roasted capsicum, combine well, then remove from the heat.

To serve, pile the capsicum and eggplant mixture into the centre of serving plates, and arrange the chicken slices on top. Lemon Aspen Mayonnaise (see recipe page 159) is an ideal accompaniment to this dish.

BARK-WRAPPED BREAST OF GUINEA FOWL WITH WILD LIME AND BLACK RICE STUFFING

When I was 16 Ray took me to Queensland to convalesce after an illness. We stayed with my Uncle Herbie at Hervey Bay. Uncle Herbie was a wharfie and would follow the ships for several months of the year to secure work. We lived in an old Queenslander-style house one street back from the water; from the verandah you could see the mountaintops of Fraser Island. The wharfies here, as in Pyrmont, formed a close, colourful community that loved a party.

One of Herbie's best mates, Chapie, who hailed from Ivanhoe in Queensland, used to stay with us. Every morning at 5 o'clock he would sing along with the local country radio station, bellowing out his favourite songs. It was an unusual way to start the day. It was also at Hervey Bay that we saw Aboriginal men walk out a mile at low tide to catch enormous mud crabs with their bare hands. This is also where we watched the local Aboriginals cook freshly caught fish in paperbark.

Serves 6

1 1/2 cups uncooked black rice, pre-soaked in water for 3–4 hours

3 lime leaves, very finely chopped

1 brown onion, roughly chopped

1 yellow capsicum, roughly chopped

1 leek, roughly chopped

4 tablespoons Garlic and Ginger Oil (see recipe page 158)

1/4 cup wild limes, roughly chopped

salt and pepper, to taste

1/2 Chinese broccoli, cut into 5 cm lengths

6 large silver beet leaves, stems trimmed at the leaf base

6 guinea fowl breasts

vegetable oil

6 x 25 cm square sheets paperbark, pre-soaked in water for 5–10 minutes

Strain and rinse the rice well, then cook it in 2 1/2 litres of boiling salted water for 20 minutes. Drain and cool.

Sauté the lime leaves, onion, capsicum and leek in the Garlic and Ginger Oil until soft and fragrant, then add the wild limes. Stir until heated through, then remove from the heat. Combine the sauté mixture and the rice in a bowl, season with the salt and pepper and set aside.

Blanch the Chinese broccoli and silver beet leaves in boiling water, plunge into iced water and drain well, taking care not to tear the silver beet leaves.

Rub each guinea fowl breast with oil, then fill the natural fold in each breast with the stuffing, packing it in tightly. Spread each silver beet leaf out, and place a little mound of Chinese broccoli in the centre. Set a guinea fowl breast over the pile of broccoli, then wrap the whole breast tightly in the silver beet. Roll the silver beet-covered breasts in the paperbark to form a cylindrical parcel, and tie at each end with kitchen twine like a bonbon.

Bake the paperbark parcels at 170°C for 10–15 minutes, then pull the centre of the bonbons open a little and bake for a further 5 minutes to brown the breast. Alternatively, brown the opened parcels under the grill. Remove from the heat and serve. This dish is delicious served with Chicken and Wild Lime Jus (see recipe page 173).

MAGPIE GOOSE AND BABY SPINACH SALAD WITH DAVIDSON PLUM DRESSING

This recipe brings back memories of my father. If he was on the evening shift and had the day to himself, he'd get up early and go to Paddy's Market (now the site of the Sydney Entertainment Centre) to buy exotic vegetables and poultry. Poultry, being expensive, was a luxury, so when Abe had a rare win on the horses he would come back with a live bird and take it to our minuscule bathroom cum laundry and toilet. After it had met its fate he would dress it, hang it in the kitchen, then scoot off to the pub for a few schooners.

When my mother came home she would inspect the bathroom like a policeman at a crime scene. There would be blood everywhere, splattered over the walls and the bath. If it had been a real struggle there would even be a sort of Red Poles of blood and feathers on the ceiling. As she began to scrub, Edna wondered whether it was all worth it. We thought so. With my father's magic culinary touch, it always tasted delicious!

1 roasted magpie goose or	DAVIDSON PLUM DRESSING:
size 18 goose or duck	6 Davidson plums or 6 hard, unripe blood plums
250 g bean sprouts	halved and stones removed
1 bunch baby spinach, washed	2 cups goose (or chicken) stock
1 punnet shiitake mushrooms, thinly sliced	4 tablespoons honey
1 punnet straw mushrooms, trimmed	1 tablespoon ginger, chopped
1 bunch endive, trimmed	2 tablespoons soy sauce
3 tablespoons pink pickled ginger	1/2 cup dry red wine
1 cup shredded coconut, lightly roasted	2 tablespoons brown sugar
	1 chilli, de-seeded and finely chopped
	salt and pepper, to taste

To make the dressing, place all of the ingredients in a saucepan and simmer for 5 minutes or until the plums are soft. Remove from the heat and cool, then purée in a blender.

Remove the flesh from the goose carcase. Shred the meat into a salad bowl, then add the bean sprouts, baby spinach, shitake mushrooms, straw mushrooms and endive. Toss the dressing through and garnish with the ginger and coconut.

Serves 4 as a light lunch or 6 as a starter.

STIR FRIED EMU WITH ASIAN GREENS AND NASHI PEARS

800 g emu

2 tablespoons olive oil

6 nashi pears

MARINADE

200 ml red wine

100 ml olive oil

1/2 knob ginger, chopped

2 chillies, chopped

2 cloves garlic, chopped

SAUCE:

1/2 cup soy sauce

1/2 cup brown sugar

4 cups water

4 tablespoons ginger, chopped

1/2 cup malt vinegar

4 tablespoons quandong kernels

2 tablespoons vegetable oil

3 cups red wine

2 teaspoons cornflour

VEGETABLES:

200 g snow peas

1 Spanish onion, sliced

1/2 punnet oyster mushrooms

1 red capsicum, sliced

1 yellow capsicum, sliced

10 baby bok choy, washed and trimmed

Slice the emu into pieces of about 5 cm. Combine marinade ingredients and pour over the emu. Marinade overnight.

Place the soy sauce, sugar, water, ginger and vinegar in a saucepan and bring to the boil. Reduce by half.

Roast the quandong kernels in a very hot pan with vegetable oil. Toss until the kernels turn black. Don't worry if they have a burnt smell. Crush the kernels in a mortar and pestle.

Add the crushed kernels to the soy sauce mixture, bring back to the boil and reduce by a quarter. Mix in the cornflour and allow the sauce to thicken.

Strain the emu from the marinade. Heat olive oil in a frying pan and sauté the emu until brown. Add the vegetables and continue sautéeing until the bok choy starts to soften. Add some sauce to moisten. Serve with sliced nashi pear.

CHICKEN BREAST WITH NATIVE ANISEED AND PEPPERLEAF CRUST

Serves 6

100 ml oil

2 tablespoons native aniseed

2 tablespoons native pepperleaf

6 corn-fed chicken breasts

3 bunches baby bok choy

PARSNIP POTATO MASH:

1 kg medium potatoes

1 kg medium parsnips

2 cloves garlic, peeled

20 g butter

salt and pepper

Combine the oil, aniseed and pepperleaf to form a loose paste, and coat the chicken breasts with it. Place in a baking dish and roast at 200°C for 15–20 minutes or until cooked.

Peel potatoes and parsnips, chop roughly and place in a pot of water with the garlic. Bring to the boil and simmer till cooked. Drain well and mash with butter, salt and pepper.

Serve the chicken with blanched baby bok choy and the mash of parsnips and potatoes. Chicken and Wild Lime Jus (see recipe page 173) is also good served with this dish.

TWICE COOKED CRISPY DUCK WITH CHINESE BROCCOLI AND DAVIDSON PLUM SAUCE

When I was in third class at St Mary's Cathedral my best friends were Cherry and Lily Lo. I loved going to their house because the food was so interesting. My first recollection of Chinese cabbage was it being served with fresh egg noodles that Mrs Lo had just made. She spent her whole life in the kitchen. She had somebody to help her with the house above the shop but she did all the cooking. I can remember having this beautiful stir-fried cabbage with ginger, lots of garlic and the noodles. I thought I'd died and gone to heaven!

Mrs Lo always gave me a little parcel to take home, which Ray, John and Dad used to drool over. It was at Mrs Lo's that I had Chinese gooseberries for the first time and I brought some home to the family. They thought this was the most exotic fruit in the world, remember that this was still the fifties and most people had never even heard of kiwi fruit.

The Lo family moved away when I was in fifth class and I was devastated; I missed them terribly. I also missed their food and the wonderful atmosphere of Chinatown where they lived.

Serves 6

3 x size 15 ducks

6 small to medium whole onions, peeled

6 cloves garlic, peeled

3 x 2.5 cm knobs ginger, peeled

6 star anise

vegetable oil

6 tablespoons hoisin sauce

2 tablespoons balsamic vinegar

2 bunches Chinese broccoli

coriander

PLUM SAUCE:

2 cloves garlic, roughly chopped

1 chilli, de-seeded and roughly chopped

200 g Davidson plums

1/2 cup red wine

1/2 litre chicken stock

1/4 fresh pineapple, core removed and flesh cut into rough chunks

2 tablespoons honey

salt and pepper, to taste

Bring a large saucepan of water to the boil, take each duck by the neck and, one at a time, plunge them into the boiling water and hold them there for about 3 minutes. Remove from the water, drain and place on a baking dish. Fill the cavity of each bird with 2 onions, 2 cloves of garlic, a knob of ginger and 2 star anise. Half fill the baking tray with water, cover it tightly with foil, and bake at 200°C for about 45 minutes or until the duck is cooked i.e. when the meat comes away from the bone when a sharp knife is run between the breasts.

Carefully remove the breasts from the cooked ducks, keeping the skin on. Remove the thighs and drumsticks in one piece by cutting deeply around the thighs and through the thigh joint, once again keeping the skin on. Discard the remaining carcase.

To MAKE THE SAUCE, combine the garlic, chilli, plums and red wine in a saucepan and bring to the boil over medium heat. Cook until the liquid has reduced by half. Add the chicken stock and continue boiling until the liquid has reduced by a further third. Add the pineapple and honey to the mixture, season with a little salt and pepper, then purée in a blender.

Thirty minutes before serving time, fry the duck pieces in about 1 cm of oil for 2–3 minutes on each side or until the skin is crispy. Drain well and pat off any excess oil with kitchen paper. Arrange the duck pieces on a baking tray and cover each piece with the combined hoisin sauce and balsamic vinegar. Bake at 250°C for 10 minutes or until the skin is crispy and the duck is warmed through.

A few minutes before the duck is ready, warm the sauce and blanch the Chinese broccoli in boiling water.

To serve, cut the breast pieces in half and cut the drumstick from the thigh, giving four pieces per person. Arrange a bed of Chinese broccoli and pour over some plum sauce. Place the duck pieces on top and garnish with coriander.

GUINEA FOWL ON KUMARA AND PARSNIP GALLETTES WITH PARCELS

Serves 6

3 guinea fowls

Chicken Stock (see recipe page 170)

BUNJA NUT AND WARRIGAL GREEN STUFFING:

2 Spanish onions, finely chopped

2 cloves garlic, finely chopped

1 knob ginger, finely chopped

100 g bunya nuts, chopped

2 lemons, zest only

100 g butter

750 g warrigal greens

1 1/2 teaspoons aniseed myrtle

salt and pepper

GUINEA FOWL PARCELS:

1 carrot, peeled and diced

1 onion, peeled and diced

1 celery stick, diced

12 guinea fowl legs (deboned)

30 ml Garlic and Ginger oil
   (see recipe page 158)

1/2 bunch silver beet,
   white stalks removed

1 1/2 teaspoons aniseed mrytle

3 leek leaves, (blanched and cut into strips)

KUMARA AND PARSNIP GALLETTES:

1 medium kumara potato, peeled

4 medium parsnips, peeled

4 eggs

300 ml fresh cream

2 teaspoons native aniseed

Cut the guinea fowls in half through the breast bone and remove the breast and leg from each side. Remove all the bones other than the leg bone. To make the stuffing, sauté the onion, garlic, lemon zest and bunja nuts in butter until the onion has softened. Add the warrigal greens and cook until tender. Remove from heat and season with aniseed myrtle and salt and pepper.Stuff the guinea fowl breasts with the mixture. Bake the guinea fowl at 170°C for 15–20 minutes.

TO MAKE THE PARCELS, mince the guinea fowl legs and set aside. Sauté carrots, onion and celery in Garlic and Ginger Oil. Combine meat, vegetables and native aniseed myrtle. Mix well. Blanch the silver beet. Lay pieces of silver beet flat and and place tablespoons of the mixture on each piece. Fold to make little parcels and tie with leek strips to secure.

TO MAKE THE GALLETTES, slice the kumara and parsnips with a mandolin to about 2 cm thick. Grease 6 tartlet moulds and place one layer of parsnip followed by 1 layer of kumara in each. Sprinkle with native aniseed and repeat layers three times. Cover with foil and bake in a moderate oven for about 10–15 minutes or until cooked through.

Heat the Chicken Stock. Place one gallette in the centre of each plate. On top of the gallette place a guinea fowl breast then surround with three parcels. Pour over the hot stock.

EMU FILLET AND PEARS WRAPPED IN PANCETTA WITH PEAR VINAIGRETTE

Serves 6–8

1.5 kg emu fan fillets

3–4 hard pears

18–24 slices pancetta

1 coral lettuce, broken into pieces

1/2 bunch rocket, broken into pieces

MARINADE:

6 cloves garlic, roughly chopped

6 sprigs lemon thyme

750 ml olive oil

300 ml red wine

8 crushed pepper berries

100 ml balsamic vinegar

PEAR VINAIGRETTE:

1 pear, unpeeled

200 ml balsamic vinegar

2 tablespoons honey

500 ml good quality olive oil

TO MAKE THE MARINADE, combine all of the ingredients in a bowl. Place the emu in the marinade, cover and refrigerate for at least 24 hours before cooking. For the best results and flavour leave for up to 72 hours.

TO MAKE THE VINAIGRETTE, cut the pear in half lengthways, remove the core and cut the pieces in halves again. Combine the pear pieces, balsamic vinegar and honey in a saucepan, bring to the boil, reduce the heat and simmer gently until the pear softens. Remove from the heat and purée. Cool, and beat through the olive oil.

Peel and core the hard pears. Cut each pear in half lengthways, then cut each half into 3 pieces lengthways. Wrap each pear piece in pancetta and secure with a toothpick. Remove the emu from the marinade and place in a frying pan with the wrapped pears. Sear on high heat until the emu is medium rare and the pancetta is crisp. Take care not to overcook. Remove from the heat and rest for 3 minutes to let the juices run free. Reheat very quickly in the pan just before serving if necessary.

To serve, toss the dressing through the coral lettuce and rocket, reserving a little to drizzle over the emu. Slice the emu into bite-sized pieces and arrange on serving plates with the pancetta-wrapped pears and the salad. Drizzle the reserved dressing over.

ROASTED DUCK BREAST WITH ROSELLA BUD CONFIT, ESCHALLOTS AND BABY BOK CHOY

Serves 6

4–6 duck breasts, deboned, skin left on

6 pieces medium-sized bok choy, halved lengthways

ROSELLA BUD CONFIT:

butter

300 g rosella buds

4 medium beetroots, cut into thin strips

2 medium onions, finely chopped

200 g caster sugar

300 ml red wine

300 ml red wine vinegar

300 ml duck or chicken stock

salt and pepper, to taste

ESCHALLOTS:

30 eschallots, approximately, peeled

75 g butter

4 cloves garlic, roughly chopped

2 tablespoons turmeric

500 ml white wine vinegar

100 ml duck or chicken stock

200 g caster sugar

salt and pepper, to taste

TO MAKE THE CONFIT, melt a little butter over low heat in a large, heavy-based saucepan. Add the rosella buds, beetroots and onions and cook for 3 minutes or until the onion becomes clear and the other ingredients start to soften.

Add the sugar, red wine, red wine vinegar and stock, bring to the boil and simmer for 5–8 minutes or until the rosella buds are tender. Strain the mixture into another saucepan, reserving the rosella buds, beetroot and onion. Simmer the remaining liquid until it has reduced by one-third. Return the rosella bud mixture to the liquid, stir through and season to taste.

TO MAKE THE ESCHALLOTS, combine all of the ingredients in a saucepan, bring to the boil, reduce the heat and simmer gently for 30–35 minutes or until the eschallots are tender but still holding their shape nicely. Drain away most of the cooking liquid, leaving just enough to coat the eschallots.

Cook the duck and bok choy close to serving time. Score the fatty area on the duck breasts several times with a sharp knife, then fry the breasts fatty side down in a hot frying pan for 5 minutes or until most of the fat has melted off. Drain the fat away.

Arrange the duck breasts in a baking dish, fatty side up, and bake at 220°C for 8–10 minutes for medium rare or about 12–15 minutes for medium to well done. Just before the duck is cooked, blanch the bok choy in boiling water for 1–2 minutes, then remove and drain.

To serve, arrange the warm confit, eschallots and bok choy around the duck.

CHAR-GRILLED QUAIL WITH SALAD OF SNOWPEA VINE LEAVES
AND ROSELLA BUD AND SOY DRESSING PG 113

ROASTED QUAIL STUFFED WITH SPINACH AND BUNYA NUTS AND SERVED WITH RISOTTO CAKES AND RIBBERRY JUS

Serves 6

6 tunnel-boned quails
(ask your supplier to do this)

RISOTTO CAKES:

1 onion, finely chopped

1 clove garlic, finely chopped

2 teaspoons ginger, finely chopped

25 g butter

2 cups arborio rice

1 kaffir lime leaf

4 cups boiling chicken stock

50 g parmesan cheese

2 teaspoons cumin

juice and finely chopped zest of 1 lime

RIBBERRY JUS:

2 cups red wine

3 cups chicken stock

1/2 cup balsamic vinegar

1 sprig thyme

2 cloves garlic, finely chopped

2 tablespoons cranberry jelly

salt and pepper, to taste

25 ribberries

SPINACH STUFFING:

1 bunch silver beet

2 Spanish onions, finely chopped

2 cloves garlic, finely chopped

2 teaspoons finely chopped fresh ginger

100 g butter

juice and finely chopped zest of 2 lemons

100 g bunya nuts, chopped

salt and pepper, to taste

MEAT STUFFING:

1 onion, finely chopped

4 teaspoons Garlic and Ginger Oil (see recipe page 158)

250 g minced veal

250 g minced pork

1/2 bunch coriander, finely chopped

salt and pepper, to taste

Prepare the risotto cakes ahead of time. Sauté the onions, garlic and ginger in the butter over medium heat in a large, heavy-based saucepan for 2–3 minutes or until soft and fragrant. Add the rice and continue to sauté, stirring constantly, for 5 minutes or until the rice grains are well coated with the fragrant butter mixture and are clear.

Add the kaffir lime leaf and the boiling chicken stock, 1 cup at a time, adding each additional portion only when the liquid in the pan has been absorbed and the rice begins to thicken. Stir every 5 minutes and avoid the temptation to overcook—the risotto is just right when all the stock has been absorbed and the rice is cooked through but still firm and separate. When the risotto is cooked, stir through the parmesan cheese, cumin and lime zest and juice. Place the mixture into a greased baking dish sized so that the rice mixture is about 2.5 cm thick.

STIR FRIED EMU WITH ASIAN GREENS AND NASHI PEARS PG 103

Set aside to cool, then place in the refrigerator for 10 minutes or until firm enough to hold its own shape when cut and fried.

TO MAKE THE RIBBERRY JUS, place the red wine in a saucepan, bring to the boil, reduce the heat and simmer until reduced by half. Add the chicken stock, balsamic vinegar, cranberry jelly, thyme and garlic and simmer until it reduces again by one-third. Season with the salt and pepper, add the ribberries and remove from the heat.

TO MAKE THE SPINACH STUFFING, wash, destalk and roughly chop the silver beet. Sauté the Spanish onions, garlic and ginger in the butter until the onion is soft and clear, then add the silver beet and continue to sauté for about 5 minutes or until the silver beet is soft. Remove from the heat, then stir through the lemon juice and zest, bunya nuts and salt and pepper.

TO MAKE THE MEAT STUFFING, sauté the onion in the Garlic and Ginger Oil until well softened, then remove from the heat and combine with the minced meats, coriander and salt and pepper.

Divide both stuffings into 8 equal portions. Flatten each minced meat portion into a round shape on the palm of your hand and place a portion of spinach stuffing in the centre—the spinach should be about the size and shape of a golf ball. Encase the spinach ball with the minced meat. Insert a ball of spinach and meat stuffing into the cavity of each quail, taking care not to break the skin and making sure the stuffing is firmly packed. Brown the quails on all sides in a hot, lightly oiled frying pan (use tongs to turn the quails but, once again, take care not to break the skin). Place in a baking dish and bake at 200°C for 15 minutes or until cooked through.

While the quail is cooking, finish making the risotto cakes by cutting the cooled risotto mixture into 6 square or circular shapes and frying each side in hot oil until golden brown and warmed through. Drain the cakes well on kitchen paper and keep warm at the bottom of the oven for a few minutes if necessary.

To serve, place a cooked quail on a risotto cake and ladle the ribberry jus over the top.

CHAR-GRILLED QUAIL WITH SALAD OF SNOWPEA VINE LEAVES AND ROSELLA BUD AND SOY DRESSING

Serves 6.

6 quails, boned and flattened
(ask your poultry supplier to do this)
18 baby corn cobs
18 rosella buds
1/4 cup hoisin sauce
1/4 cup balsamic vinegar
SAUCE:
1/2 cup malt vinegar
4 tablespoons green ginger,
finely chopped

4 cups water
1/2 cup soy sauce
1/2 cup brown sugar
1 medium onion, peeled and quartered
1 cup rosella buds
1 tablespoon lime juice
1 tablespoon fish sauce
1 teaspoon cornflour (optional)
4 handfuls snowpea vine leaves

To make the sauce, place the malt vinegar, ginger, water, soy sauce, brown sugar, onion, rosella buds, lime juice and fish sauce in a saucepan and bring to the boil. Simmer for 5 minutes then strain. To thicken the sauce, mix a tablespoon of the sauce into the cornflour, stirring to remove any lumps. Pour the cornflour into the sauce and heat gently, stirring until the sauce covers the back of a spoon. Set aside and reheat to serve.

Mix together the hoisin sauce and balsamic vinegar. Brush the quails, baby corn cobs and rosella buds with the hoisin and balsamic. Char grill for 5 minutes or until medium cooked, turning once.

Divide the snowpea vine leaves into 6 portions. Arrange the leaves in the centre of each plate with the corn cobs. Sit the quail on top. Pour sauce around each plate and garnish with rosella buds.

MOROCCAN SPICED CHICKEN WITH LEMON ASPEN JUS AND LENTILS

The chicken is best marinated overnight, while the jus can be made up to a day ahead.

Serves 6

6 chicken breasts

MARINADE:

450 ml olive oil

100 ml lemon juice

2 x 2.5 cm knobs ginger, roughly chopped

5 cloves garlic, roughly chopped

2 tablespoons turmeric

1 bunch coriander, roughly chopped

1 tablespoon ginger powder

1 tablespoon cumin

2 chillies, de-seeded and roughly chopped

LEMON ASPEN JUS:

3 litres chicken stock

3 cloves bruised garlic

12 lemon aspen fruit, cores removed

juice of 1 lemon

1 tablespoon cumin

1 chilli, de-seeded and chopped

1/2 bunch coriander, roughly chopped

salt and pepper, to taste

cornflour, optional

LENTILS:

2 cups brown lentils

1 onion, finely chopped

4 tablespoons Garlic and Ginger Oil
  (see recipe page 158)

2 cups water

1/2 bunch coriander, roughly chopped

1 red capsicum, finely chopped

1 tablespoon cumin

Combine all of the marinade ingredients in a large bowl, place the chicken breasts in it, cover and marinate in the refrigerator overnight.

TO MAKE THE LEMON ASPEN JUS, heat the stock, garlic and lemon aspens in a saucepan and simmer steadily for five minutes. Remove garlic and continue to simmer until the liquid has reduced by two-thirds. Stir in the lemon juice, cumin, chilli and coriander and season with the salt and pepper. For a thicker sauce, mix a little cornflour with 1 tablespoon of water to form a loose paste, and stir this into the sauce. Return to the boil. You can prepare the sauce up to a day ahead, then reheat.

TO MAKE THE LENTILS, pour boiling water over the lentils and soak for 30 minutes. Drain, rinse and set aside. Sauté the onion in the Garlic and Ginger Oil until barely soft, then add the lentils and the water and cook for 10–15 minutes, stirring occasionally, until the water has been absorbed and the lentils are soft but still holding their shape.

While the lentils are cooking, remove the chicken from the marinade and sear on all sides in a hot frying pan brushed with vegetable oil. Bake the chicken at 180°C for 15 minutes or until cooked through.

When the lentils are cooked, add the coriander, red capsicum and cumin and stir until well heated.

To serve, place the lentils on a pool of jus and top with the chicken breasts. This dish is delicious served with some crispy pappadums.

CHICKEN BREAST WITH COUS-COUS AND BRAISED RADICCHIO

Serves 6

6 corn-fed chicken breasts

10 g butter

2 cloves garlic, finely crushed

1 radicchio lettuce, leaves separated

200 ml chicken stock

Cous-cous:

2 cups chicken stock

2 cups cous-cous

1 chilli, de-seeded and finely chopped

1 Spanish onion, finely diced

1/2 cup red capsicum, finely diced

1/2 cup yellow capsicum, finely diced

1/2 bunch coriander, finely chopped

salt and pepper, to taste

2 tablespoons Garlic and Ginger Oil
 (see recipe page 158)

Chicken and Wild Lime Jus (see recipe page 173)

To make the cous-cous, bring the chicken stock to the boil in a pan, then pour over the cous-cous. Let stand for about 3 minutes then, with a fork in each hand, beat the cous-cous lightly until it separates nicely into fluffy grains.

Sauté the chilli, onion, capsicum, coriander, salt and pepper in the Garlic and Ginger Oil for 1–2 minutes or until fragrant and barely softened, then add them to the cous-cous and mix through well. Cover the bowl with clingwrap and stand in a warm place until ready to serve or slowly warm in pan.

Bake the chicken breasts at 180°C for about 15 minutes or until cooked through.

Melt the butter in a frying pan over low heat, then add the garlic and radicchio leaves. Sauté for about 1 minute, then add the chicken stock and cook over low heat until the leaves are soft but not soggy. Remove the leaves and serve immediately.

Sauce the serving plates with Chicken and Wild Lime Jus, reserving enough sauce to drizzle a little over the chicken, top with cous-cous and then a bed of radicchio. Arrange the chicken breasts on top.

AT

Credibility Luncheons

At the first Edna's Table we used to have a Credibility Luncheon. This involved a lot of media people who came and did what they do best—get very drunk! As we weren't open on a Monday night the lunch had the possibility of running on into the late hours, and it often did. A Credibility Lunch only had credibility if it went until midnight. Mr Lunch-a-Lot, Mike Carlton, headed the bill every year. Nigel Milan from 2GB was the host and, when he left, Geoffrey Duncan. It was packed with the who's who of the print and electronic journalistic world—everyone wanted to come because it was so much fun. There would be credibility awards and it was very tongue in cheek. I remember Kerri-Anne Kennerley getting her first award, and a young Ann Sanders, and Barry Humphries coming once as Les Patterson. Paul Murphy, George Negus, the late Robert Haupt, Germaine Greer—you name the brightest stars in journalism and they were there.

We were very nervous about the first one because food critic Leo Schofield was coming, and we'd never done an event like this. We ordered a great amount of veal and Raymond was going to get up early on Sunday and trim it. I ordered a whole new lot of Wedgwood cups and saucers but, come Saturday, I couldn't find them. Come Sunday, Raymond couldn't find the veal. He was beginning to panic—he couldn't prepare meat that didn't exist. On Monday we had to get in more veal and Abe and Edna helped him trim it. I managed to courier over new crockery and all went well with the lunch.

The restaurant had a cool room in the basement as well as a storeroom for wine. We had this delightful Tamil on our staff, a fully fledged chartered accountant who was working as a kitchen hand because of his language problems. He was very proud and very educated. We had no idea what had happened to the mysterious disappearing veal and china but two weeks later there was a terrible smell coming from the wine cellar. We went to investigate and found the boxes of veal. They had been packed in Cryovac, so it had taken a long time for the smell to come through. We found the cups and saucers in the cool room. Our Tamil had even less English than we had imagined; he had just signed the delivery dockets and put the boxes away having no idea of what was in them.

POACHED VEAL WRAPPED IN PAPERBARK WITH PALMASAMI AND WITLOF

Serves 6

1.2 kg piece veal strip loin,
   cut into 6 portions
1 cup Palmasami (see recipe page 165)
6 large silver beet leaves
1 teaspoon pepperleaf
salt, to taste
6 sheets 30 cm x 38 cm sheets paperbark,
   pre-soaked in water for 10 minutes

3 witlof lettuces, halved
Garlic and Ginger Oil (see recipe page 158)
Sauce:
1 cup veal jus or 1 cup beef stock (see recipes
   pages 169-172) to which 1 tablespoon redcurrant jelly
   and 1 clove garlic has been added
1 cup Pandana Leaf Sauce (see recipe page 161)
1/2 teaspoon native thyme

Slice a pocket into each piece of veal. Place 2 tablespoons of the Palmasami into each pocket.

Blanch the silver beet leaves in boiling water for about 10 seconds, then plunge into iced water and pat dry, taking care to leave them whole. Remove the white stalks at the base of the leaves, then spread them out on a board or similar surface.

Bring a poaching kettle or a large pot of water to the boil, and season with the pepperleaf and salt. Meanwhile, wrap the veal loins tightly in the silver beet leaves. Place each veal parcel on the centre of a paperbark sheet, bring the edges of the paperbark up, and tie tightly with kitchen twine to form little parcels. Poach the veal parcels, covered, in the steadily simmering water for 10–15 minutes. Remove the parcels, and sit them on a teatowel to drain.

Fry the witlof halves in the Garlic and Ginger Oil for 5 minutes.

To make the sauce, bring the veal jus, Pandana Leaf Sauce and native thyme to the boil, then remove from the heat.

Unwrap the veal parcels and remove the silver beet layer. Pour the sauce over the veal, the paperbark will hold it in. Serve with the fried witlof.

WARM SALAD OF KANGAROO, CARAMELISED ESCHALLOTS AND BABY BEETROOT WITH GINGER AND ROSELLA BUD DRESSING

Serves 6

18 baby beetroot, stalks removed

6 strip loins kangaroo

vegetable oil

2 Spanish onions, cut into 1 cm thick slices

30 snow peas

1 punnet straw mushrooms

1 cos lettuce, torn into 5 cm lengths

18 rocket leaves

6 sprigs purple Thai basil

CARAMELISED ESCHALLOTS:

18 yellow eschallots

30 g butter

2 cloves garlic

1 tablespoons turmeric

250 ml white wine vinegar

50 ml duck or chicken stock

100 g caster sugar

salt and pepper, to taste

ROSELLA BUD AND GINGER DRESSING:

600 ml Kangaroo Jus (see recipe page 172)

1 x 4 cm knob ginger, roughly chopped

1 tablespoon ginger powder

3 cups rosella buds

salt and pepper, to taste

Scrub the beetroot well and place in a baking dish filled with 3 cm of water. Bake at 200°C for 30–40 minutes or until a skewer can be easily inserted.

TO MAKE THE CARAMELISED ESCHALLOTS, place all of the ingredients in a saucepan, bring to the boil and simmer gently for 20 minutes or until the eschallots are tender but still holding their shape nicely. Drain away most of the cooking liquid, leaving just enough to coat the eschallots.

TO MAKE THE DRESSING, heat the Kangaroo Jus, and gingers in a saucepan, bring to the boil and add the rosella buds. Reduce the heat and simmer for 2–3 minutes, then remove from the heat and purée in a blender. Season to taste.

Slice each kangaroo loin diagonally into 4 pieces. Heat the oil in a frying pan until it is smoking, then add the kangaroo pieces and the onion and cook for 2–3 minutes or until the meat is browned on one side. Add the beetroot and eschallots, and turn the kangaroo to brown on the other side. Add the snow peas and mushrooms and toss them through, then pour in the dressing. Bring to the boil, remove from the heat. Toss the cos lettuce through.

To serve, arrange 3 rocket leaves on each serving plate and pile the salad over, using tongs to ensure that the servings are evenly apportioned. Garnish with the Thai basil.

CHAR-GRILLED FILLET OF KANGAROO WITH BEETROOT RISOTTO PG 122

LAMB POACHED IN PAPERBARK WITH LEMON MYRTLE CURRY SAUCE

Serves 6

6 large silver beet leaves

1/2 bunch ky choy

6 lamb fillets or lamb loins

salt and pepper, to taste

1 tablespoon curry powder

1 teaspoon fennel seeds

1 teaspoon caraway seeds

1 teaspoon salt, extra

6 sheets 30 cm x 38 cm paperbark, pre-soaked in water for 10 minutes

Lemon Myrtle and Lime Curry Sauce (see recipe page 166)

1 1/2 cups macadamia nuts, roasted and roughly chopped

Blanch each silver beet leaf and the ky choy in boiling water for about 10 seconds, then plunge in iced water and pat dry, taking care to leave the silver beet leaves whole. Spread the silver beet leaves out, and remove the white stems at the base of each leaf. Divide the ky choy into 6 portions, placing one portion in the centre of each silver beet leaf.

Cut the lamb fillets in half horizontally, giving two shorter pieces, then place these on the ky choy. Season with salt and pepper.

Bring a poaching kettle or a large pot of water to the boil, and season with the curry powder, fennel seeds, caraway seeds and extra salt. Meanwhile, wrap the lamb fillets tightly in the silver beet leaves. Place each lamb parcel on the centre of a paperbark sheet, bring the edges of the paperbark up and tie tightly with kitchen twine to form little parcels. Poach the lamb parcels, covered, in the steadily simmering water for 10–15 minutes. Remove the parcels, and sit them on a teatowel to drain.

Place the lamb parcels on serving plates, open up the paperbark and remove the silver beet layer. Top with hot Lemon and Myrtle Curry Sauce and sprinkle with the crushed macadamia nuts. This dish can be served with new potatoes and rocket lettuce leaves, or with steamed jasmine rice.

CHAR-GRILLED KANGAROO FILLET WITH JERUSALEM ARTICHOKE COMPOTE AND ILLAWARRA PLUM SALSA PG 119

CHAR-GRILLED VENISON LOIN WITH CHEESEFRUIT AND EGGPLANT RISOTTO AND NATIVE THYME JUS

Serves 6

6 x 200 g portions of venison loin

600 ml Beef Jus (see recipe page 173)

1 tablespoon native thyme

CHEESEFRUIT AND EGGPLANT RISOTTO:

5 cups water

3 cloves garlic, finely chopped

2 x 4 cm knobs ginger, finely chopped

2 medium onions, finely chopped

20 g butter

3 cups arborio rice

1 large eggplant, cut into 1 cm dice

2 cups Cheesefruit Sauce (see recipe page 162)

salt and pepper, to taste

To make the risotto, put the water on to boil. In a separate, heavy-based saucepan sauté the garlic, ginger and onions in the butter until fragrant and well softened. Add the rice and eggplant and continue to sauté for 2–3 minutes more or until the rice becomes translucent. Add the boiling water and cook at a steady simmer, stirring frequently, until the water has been absorbed. Add the Cheesefruit Sauce and continue to cook over low heat, stirring frequently, until the rice is cooked through but still firm and holding its shape. Remove from the heat and season to taste.

Cook the venison on a char grill or in a hot, lightly oiled pan. Sear on all sides first, then reduce the heat and cook for 5–8 minutes or until the meat is cooked to your preference. Remove from the heat and rest for a few minutes.

Just before serving, place the Beef Jus and native thyme in a pan and bring to the boil. Remove from the heat.

To serve, arrange the venison on top of the risotto on each serving plate, then cover with a generous amount of hot jus.

JENNICE IN PAPUA NEW GUINEA

DESS

E R T S

WATTLE SEED CREME BRULEE

Serves 6
(at 200 ml
per brulée).

700 ml cream	10 egg yolks
1 tablespoon wattle seeds	120 g caster sugar
1 vanilla bean, split lengthwise	

Place the cream, wattle seeds and vanilla bean in a saucepan and cook over low heat. While this is heating, whisk together the egg yolks and sugar in a large, heatproof mixing bowl until light, fluffy and well combined. When the cream mixture is just at boiling point, begin adding it, bit by bit, to the egg yolk and sugar mixture, whisking constantly as you do so. Once complete, let this mixture stand for 3–4 minutes until it has settled and is no longer frothy. Remove the vanilla bean then pour the mixture into 6 brulée moulds or small ovenproof ramekins.

Half fill a baking dish with water to make a 'bain-marie', arrange the brulées in it, and seal the baking dish tightly with aluminium foil. Bake at 120°C for about 30 minutes, or until the brulée mixture is well thickened, to the consistency of a light set custard. Remove from the oven, cool and refrigerate.

Serve with fresh or poached fruit.

WILD LIME AND GINGER CREME BRULEE

Serves 6

1/2 cup wild limes	800 ml thickened cream
1 cup liquid glucose	1 tablespooon fresh grated ginger
juice and zest of 4 limes	12 egg yolks
2 vanilla beans, 1 scraped with a	4 tablespoons caster sugar
serrated knife, 1 split lengthwise	1 tablespoon ground ginger

Blanch the wild limes in boiling water, then plunge in iced water. Strain and set aside. Set the blanching water aside to use again. Place the glucose, 1/2 cup of the blanching water, the juice and zest of two limes and the scraped vanilla bean into a saucepan, bring to the boil and cook for three minutes. Remove from the heat and divide the mixture evenly into 6 brulée moulds or small ramekins—the mixture should cover the bottom of each mould.

Combine the cream, ginger, split vanilla bean and lime juice and zest in a saucepan and bring just to boiling point. While this is heating, whisk the egg yolks and caster sugar in a stainless steel bowl or saucepan until light, fluffy and well combined. Set the bowl over a pot of boiling water and whisk steadily for about 10 minutes or until the mixture is thick enough to resist whisking and clings to the whisk in strands when it is drawn away from the bowl.

While still whisking slowly pour in the hot cream mixture. When all the cream has been added, continue whisking the mixture over the hot water with a wooden spoon until it is smooth, thick and spreadable (about 10–15 minutes). Remove the vanilla bean. Cool by setting the bowl over some crushed ice, then pour it slowly into the moulds over the top of the glucose and lime mixture. Stand in the refrigerator until set and ready to serve.

SPICED QUANDONG AND LYCHEE COMPOTE WITH TUILE BISCUITS

Serves 6–8

3 star anise
1 cinnamon stick
1 vanilla bean
1/2 cup honey (preferably blue gum)
1/4 cup orange blossom flower water
1/2 cup white wine
zest and juice of 2 oranges
zest and juice of 2 limes

2 cups quandongs, de-seeded and roughly chopped
2 cups lychees, peeled, de-seeded and halved

TUILE BISCUITS:
1/2 cup icing sugar
1/2 cup plain flour
3 egg whites
90 g melted butter

Combine all of the ingredients except the quandongs and lychees in a saucepan and boil for 4–5 minutes or until the mixture is slightly reduced. Strain the mixture and reserve the zest. Return the liquid and the zest to the saucepan and bring to the boil again. Add the quandongs and cook for 3–4 minutes or until tender. Remove from the heat and leave to cool, then stir the lychees through.

TO MAKE THE TUILE BISCUITS, sift the icing sugar and flour together then add the unbeaten egg whites and melted butter. Mix thoroughly and leave to cool in the refrigerator. Let stand for two hours. When cool, spread the tuile mixture very thinly into oval shapes about 10 cm x 5 cm on a lightly greased baking tray. Bake at 150°C for 5 minutes or until golden.

When the tuiles are removed from the oven they will be quite pliable. Quickly shape them into cones or cylinders using a flat-bladed knife and your fingers. The tuiles will cool and harden into this shape.

To serve the compote, top with a tuile and a dollop of thick fresh cream or crème fraîche on the side.

NATIVE PEPPERMINT BAVAROIS WITH WILD LIME JUS

Serves 8

4 cups cream

250 g caster sugar

5 egg yolks

5 teaspoons gelatin

1 tablespoon native peppermint

1/2 teaspoon native peppermint oil

WILD LIME JUS:

1 cup wild limes

250 ml sugar syrup (made by mixing 1 cup sugar with
1 cup water, then boiling until the sugar dissolves)

250 ml liquid glucose

juice and zest of 4 limes

Place half of the cream in a small saucepan and cook over low heat until it is just at boiling point. Make sure the cream doesn't boil over—remove and replace it on the heat if necessary.

In a stainless steel bowl, whisk the sugar and egg yolks until light and fluffy, then set the bowl over a saucepan of boiling water and continue whisking vigorously, following an imaginary figure 8-shape with the whisk in the bowl. When the mixture is thick enough to hold the shape (i.e. it is a sabayon) whisk in the hot cream, which should be just at boiling point, a little at a time. When it is all added, stir over the heat until the mixture is thick enough to coat the back of a spoon when it is drawn out of the mixture. The mixture is now a crème anglaise.

Sprinkle the gelatin onto the hot anglaise and stir until dissolved. Set aside to cool.

Very lightly grease 6–8 small ramekins or bavarois moulds with unsalted butter. Whip the remaining half of the cream until it forms soft peaks, do not overbeat. When half-whipped, add the native peppermint and continue whisking. Fold the whipped cream gently but thoroughly into the cooled anglaise then pour into the greased moulds. Cover the moulds with greaseproof paper and place in the refrigerator to set.

TO MAKE THE WILD LIME JUS, blanch the wild limes in boiling water then plunge into iced water. Repeat this procedure 4 times, using fresh water each time, to remove the bitterness. Combine the sugar syrup, glucose and lime juice and zest in a saucepan and simmer over low heat for 5 minutes. Add the wild limes, remove from heat and set aside to cool.

To serve, turn out the bavarois as you would a jelly, by dipping the moulds into hot water for a moment then upending them onto a plate into a pool of the wild lime jus.

PYRMONT

SOUR CREAM PUDDING WITH BLACK APPLE AND MUNTHARI BERRIES

Serves 6–8

BLACK APPLE AND MUNTHARI BERRY TOPPING:

1 cup red wine

1/2 cup sugar

1/2 cup water

1/2 vanilla bean

1 cinnamon stick

6 black apples, peeled, cored and
   cut into thick segments

1 cup munthari berries

SOUR CREAM PUDDING:

225 g butter

1 cup sugar

2 eggs

300 ml sour cream

2 cups plain flour

1 teaspoons bicarbonate of soda

1/4 teaspoon salt

1/4 teaspoon vanilla

1 tablespoon cinnamon

1 teaspoon cloves

1/2 teaspoon nutmeg

TO MAKE THE BLACK APPLE AND MUNTHARI BERRY TOPPING, combine all of the ingredients except the apples and munthari berries in a saucepan, bring to the boil and simmer for about 5 minutes, stirring constantly. Add the apples and poach on a low simmer for about 10 minutes, till apples are soft. Add the munthari berries, stir, then remove the saucepan from the heat, strain and cool. When cool, spoon into the bottom of a 25 cm cake tin.

TO MAKE THE SOUR CREAM PUDDING, cream the butter and sugar together. Beat in the eggs and then beat in the sour cream, stirring until well combined. Sift together the flour, bicarbonate of soda and salt and fold into the sour cream mixture. Add the vanilla, cinnamon, cloves and nutmeg and combine well.

Pour the sour cream pudding over the top of the berries in the cake tin. Bake at 140°C for about 45 minutes. Serve with double cream, icecream or custard.

WILD LIME, LEMON AND QUANDONG TART

The first time I had quandongs was when I was staying at my sister-in-law's property at Yahgunyah, close to Warren. We used to go to Mass every Sunday at Quombone and afterwards people would bring sandwiches and turn it into a social gathering; some people had driven from far distant places to go to church. I remember someone offering me a tart that had quandong in it, and apologising about using this fruit. I remember thinking how strange it was to apologise for something that tasted so good.

Serves 6–8

TART CRUST:

150 g macadamia nuts

150 g pine nuts

150 g walnuts

50 g butter

50 g brown sugar

50 g breadcrumbs

CARAMELIZED QUANDONGS:

1/2 cup sugar

water

3 cups quandongs, roughly chopped

1/2 cup red wine

1 lime, juiced

1 tablespoon cassis or grenadine

1 vanilla bean

2 cinnamon sticks

3 star anise

1 1/2 tablespoons cornflour

WILD LIME AND LEMON CURD:

1/2 cup wild limes

150 ml lemon juice

2 lemons, zested

50 ml orange juice

1 cup caster sugar

8 egg yolks

4 whole eggs

30 g butter, cut into small cubes

TO MAKE THE TART CRUST, combine all of the ingredients in a blender or food processor and process until the mixture is thick and crumbly. Spread the mixture to about 1/2 cm thickness around the base and sides of a 25 cm flan dish, pressing the mixture firmly in place with your fingers. Place in the refrigerator to set.

TO MAKE THE CARAMELISED QUANDONGS, combine all the ingredients except the cornflour in a pan and bring to the boil. Simmer for 10 minutes then remove from the heat. Combine the cornflour with 3 tablespoons of water to form a smooth, runny paste, and stir through the hot quandong mixture. Return the saucepan to the heat and bring to the boil, stirring constantly, until all of the ingredients form a smooth syrup. Remove from the heat, cool slightly and pour into the prepared flan tin.

TO MAKE THE WILD LIME AND LEMON CURD, bring a saucepan of water to the boil, drop in the wild limes, remove immediately and plunge in a bowl of iced water. Repeat this blanching process, then set the limes aside.

In a small bowl combine the lemon juice, lemon zest, orange juice and one-fifth of the sugar. Whisk the egg yolks, whole eggs and remaining sugar in a stainless steel bowl until fluffy, place the bowl over a large saucepan of boiling water and continue to whisk vigorously until the mixture has a thick, spreadable consistency. Whisk in the lemon, lemon zest and orange mixture and continue whisking until the thick consistency is regained. Gradually whisk in the diced butter and wild limes. When the mixture is thoroughly combined and has a thick, smooth consistency, pour it into the flan dish over the quandongs. Leave the tart to set in the refrigerator for at least 1 hour before serving.

MACADAMIA NUT BISCOTTI

3 cups egg whites	3 1/2 cups plain flour
3 1/2 cups caster sugar	2 cups whole macadamia nuts

Whisk the egg whites and the sugar until the mixture forms stiff peaks. Fold through the flour, and then fold through the nuts, taking care not to overbeat the mixture as the egg whites will reliquefy. Pour the mixture into 3 well-greased loaf tins.

Bake at 120°C for 45 minutes or until the cake springs back when lightly touched in the centre. Remove from the oven and set aside to cool. Turn out the cakes, wrap them in clingwrap and place in the freezer until they are partially frozen. Remove from the freezer and slice crosswise as thinly as possible—about 2 mm in thickness.

Arrange the biscotti on a well-greased baking tray, and bake at 180°C until golden brown. Remove from the oven and store in an airtight container—they will keep for up to 2 weeks.

INDIVIDUAL BANANA AND BUNYA NUT PUDDINGS WITH LEMON MYRTLE ANGLAISE

Serves 6–8

BANANA AND BUNYA NUT PUDDINGS:

3 cups plain flour

2 cups sugar

1 teaspoon salt

1 teaspoon bicarbonate of soda

1 teaspoon cinnamon

3 eggs, beaten

1 1/2 cups oil

1 teaspoon vanilla

250 g tinned crushed pineapple, undrained

2 cups tinned pineapple rings, drained and coarsely chopped

2 cups banana, peeled and cut into approximately 1 cm cubes

2 cups bunya nuts, coarsely chopped

LEMON MYRTLE CRÈME ANGLAISE:

4 cups cream

2 tablespoons lemon myrtle

1 vanilla bean, split

10 egg yolks

250 g sugar

To make the puddings, sift together the flour, sugar, salt, bicarbonate of soda and cinnamon, then gently fold in the eggs and oil until they are well absorbed by the dry ingredients. Stir in the vanilla, crushed pineapple, pineapple rings, banana and bunya nuts until well combined.

Thoroughly grease and flour 6–8 small pudding moulds or ovenproof ramekins, and divide the mixture evenly among them. Bake at 180°C for 25 minutes or until a skewer inserted into the puddings comes out clean.

TO MAKE THE LEMON MYRTLE CRÈME ANGLAISE, combine the cream, lemon myrtle and vanilla bean in a saucepan over low heat. While this is heating, whisk the egg yolks and sugar together until light and fluffy. When the cream is just at boiling point but not actually boiling remove from the heat. Remove the vanilla bean and gradually whisk the cream into the egg and sugar mixture. When all the cream has been added, pour the mixture back into the saucepan and stir constantly over a very low heat until it is thick enough to coat the back of a spoon.

Remove from the heat, and set the saucepan into a bowl of iced water to cool, if desired, or the anglaise can be served hot. The anglaise can be reheated, however, stir constantly as you do so to avoid lumps forming.

To serve the puddings hot, pour the anglaise over the top. To serve cold, set the puddings on a pool of anglaise.

WATTLE SEED SHORTBREAD

500 g softened butter

2 cups brown sugar

1 1/2 tablespoons wattle seeds

4 1/4 cups plain flour

Cream together the butter and sugar. Beat in the wattle seeds and the flour. Roll the dough out to a 2 cm thickness, then cut into shapes. Place on a greased scone tray, and cool in the refrigerator for at least 1 hour or until the dough has firmly set.

Bake at 150°C for 10 minutes or until a pale golden colour. Serve with coffee and tea (or eat whenever you need a snack!).

GLASS BISCUITS

100 g butter

90 g glucose

180 g sugar

90 g plain flour

Melt the butter and glucose in a saucepan over a low heat. Add the sugar and plain flour and mix together well. Refrigerate the mixture until firm. Preheat oven to 150°C–170°C. Form small balls (about half the size of a golf ball) and place between two sheets of silicon paper and roll out to about 3 mm thickness. Place on an oven tray and bake for about 5 minutes until golden brown. Remove from the oven and while they are still hot cut into the desired shape. Allow to cool on a cake rack.

Serve with icecream or instead of tuiles.

WILD LIME, LEMON AND QUONDONG TART PG **141**

NECTARINE AND WILD PLUM UPSIDE DOWN CAKE WITH ORANGE MASCARPONE

TOPPING:

125 g softened butter

1 cup brown sugar

2/3 cup walnuts, roughly chopped

2/3 cup macadamia nuts, roughly chopped

1 cup caster sugar

1 cup red wine

4 Davidson plum halves

4 medium nectarines, seeds removed,
   sliced into 2 cm segments

CAKE BASE:

2 cups milk

2 eggs

2 3/4 cups brown sugar

2 3/4 cups self-raising flour

145 g softened butter

2 teaspoons nutmeg

2 teaspoons bicarbonate of soda

2 teaspoons mixed spice

1 cup macadamia nuts, roughly chopped

1 cup walnuts, roughly chopped

ORANGE MASCARPONE:

250 g mascarpone

zest and juice of 1 orange

2 capsful Grand Marnier

1 tablespoon orange blossom flower water

To make the topping, lightly grease a 25 cm round cake tin. Combine the butter, brown sugar, walnuts and macadamias in a bowl and mix well. Spread over the bottom of the cake tin with your fingers and press it down firmly.

In a saucepan, combine the caster sugar, red wine and Davidson plums. Bring to the boil, remove from the heat and strain immediately. Discard the liquid. Slice the plums and the nectarines uniformly, removing the stones, and spread the slices over the topping layer in the cake tin.

TO MAKE THE CAKE BASE, combine the milk and eggs in a bowl and whisk well. Cream the sugar and butter. Mix together with the remaining ingredients in a separate bowl, then combine with the milk and egg mixture.

Pour the cake base mixture over the topping and fruit in the cake tin, and bake at 170°C for 1 hour or until the cake springs back lightly when touched or a skewer inserted into the centre comes out clean. Turn the cake out—the topping and fruit will have combined into a delicious layer.

To make the orange mascarpone, combine all of the ingredients in a bowl and stir until smooth.

Serve the cake with dollops of Orange Mascarpone.

JENNICE AT EDNA'S TABLE II

INDIVIDUAL BLACK RICE AND MUNTHARI BERRY PUDDINGS WITH CARAMEL SAUCE

Serves 8

BLACK RICE AND MUNTHARI BERRY PUDDINGS:

1 cup sugar

1 cup water

1 tablespoon cold water, extra

6 eggs

3/4 cup sugar, extra

1 1/2 cups milk

1 cup cream

1 1/2 teaspoon vanilla essence

1 tablespoon Grand Marnier

8 tablespoons munthari berries

16 tablespoons cooked black rice

Caramel Sauce (see recipe page 165)

To make the puddings, place the sugar and water in a saucepan and bring to the boil until the mixture begins to turn golden and a toffee starts to form. To test if the toffee is ready, place a small spoonful into a glass of cold water—the toffee should set to the point where it is still sticky and hard to chew. If it sets very solid and breaks when chewed it is overcooked. Carefully add the extra water, stir well and remove from the heat.

Grease 8 x 3/4 cup capacity pudding moulds. Pour a little of the toffee mixture into each of the moulds so it forms a layer at the bottom. Cover the toffee layer with a sprinkling of munthari berries and place the moulds in the refrigerator.

Meanwhile, whisk the eggs, then add the extra sugar and the milk, cream, vanilla and Grand Marnier. Whisk together well. Pour the mixture evenly into each mould, leaving about 15 mm clear to the rim. Gently spoon 2 tablespoons of the cooked black rice into each pudding.

Half fill a baking dish with boiling water and arrange the puddings in it. Cover the dish tightly with foil and bake at 150°C for 20–25 minutes or until the puddings begin to set. Be careful not to overcook, or the pudding mixture will separate. Remove from the oven and cool at room temperature, then place the puddings in the refrigerator to chill.

To serve, carefully turn the puddings out of the moulds onto serving plates. If they do not turn out easily, dip each mould in a little hot water before tipping it up. Serve the puddings with fresh tropical fruit such as mango, papaya and banana and covered in caramel sauce.

ROSELLA BUD AND RICOTTA CAKE WITH MACADAMIA PRALINE

MACADAMIA PRALINE:

1/2 cup macadamia nuts, crushed into gravel-sized pieces

1 cup sugar

1 cup water

CAKE CRUST:

3 1/4 cups plain flour

3 teaspoons baking powder

2/3 cup brown sugar

1 cup almond meal

1 egg, lightly beaten

1 teaspoon vanilla essence

250 g cold butter

ROSELLA BUDS:

2 cups rosella buds

1 cup red wine

1/2 cup sugar

1 cinnamon stick

zest and juice of 1 lime

FILLING:

600 g ricotta cheese, drained

1 cup caster sugar

100 g dark chocolate, roughly chopped

TO MAKE THE MACADAMIA PRALINE, grease a baking tray and scatter the crushed nuts over it. Place the sugar and water in a saucepan, bring to the boil and cook for about 7 minutes or until the mixture is a dark golden colour. Remove from heat, pour the mixture over the tray of nuts and leave to set. When set, break into chunks.

TO MAKE THE CAKE CRUST, place all of the ingredients except the butter in a food processor and blend. Add the butter and blend again until the mixture has the consistency of breadcrumbs.

Lightly grease a 20 cm cake tin and press three-quarters of the mixture firmly into the base with your fingers, forming a crust about 1 1/2 cm thick. Reserve the remaining quarter of the crust mix.

TO PREPARE THE ROSELLA BUDS, combine them with the remaining ingredients in a saucepan and simmer over low heat for 5 minutes. Remove from the heat and strain, reserving the rosella buds and discarding the liquid.

TO MAKE THE FILLING, combine the ricotta cheese, caster sugar and praline chunks in a food processor and blend for 1–2 minutes, then add the chocolate. Blend again for 1–2 minutes, making sure the chocolate does not become puréed.

Fill the cake crust with the ricotta mixture to within 2 cm from the top, then spread the rosella buds over. Sprinkle the remaining crust mixture over the rosella buds. Bake at 180°C for 1 hour.

HOT AUSTRALIAN CHRISTMAS PUDDING WITH WATTLE SEED CREME ANGLAISE

125 g munthari berries	1/2 cup dark rum
60 g riberries	100 ml brandy
60 g rosella buds	3 1/2 cups self-raising four
250 g dried fruit	3 teaspoons bicarbonate of soda
100 g caster sugar	1/2 cup boiling water
250 g butter	WATTLE SEED CRÈME ANGLAISE:
600 ml milk	4 cups cream
125 g walnuts	1 tablespoon wattle seeds
250 g brown sugar	1 vanilla bean
1 teaspoon nutmeg	10 egg yolks
1/2 teaspoon ground cloves	150 g caster sugar
1 teaspoon cinnamon	

In a very large saucepan, combine all of the ingredients except the brandy, self-raising flour, bicarbonate of soda and boiling water. Bring to the boil, stirring occasionally, then simmer for 5 minutes. Remove from the heat and add the brandy, then sift in the flour and mix well. Dissolve the bicarbonate of soda in the boiling water and add to the mixture, combining thoroughly.

Grease and flour a 1.5 litre capacity pudding basin and one side of a piece of foil at least twice the size of the basin top. Fill the basin with the mixture and cover it with the foil, greased side down, folding the foil back on itself to form a large pleat in the centre so that the pudding has room to rise. Seal the foil tightly around the rim of the basin with kitchen twine. Half fill a baking dish with water, and place the pudding in the baking dish. Bake at 200°C for about 1 1/2 hours or until a skewer inserted in the centre comes out clean.

TO MAKE THE CRÈME ANGLAISE, combine the cream, wattle seeds and vanilla bean in a saucepan and cook over low heat until almost at boiling point. Remove the vanilla bean. Meanwhile, whisk the egg yolks and sugar together until light and fluffy. When the cream is at boiling point (but not boiling), gradually whisk it into the egg and sugar mixture.

Serve the pudding with either hot or cold crème anglaise. The crème anglaise can be reheated, but stir constantly as you do so or it may separate.

LEMON MYRTLE BAVAROIS
COATED IN WILD LIME JELLY

Serves 4

BAVAROIS:

5 egg yolks

200 g castor sugar

450 ml milk

15 lemon myrtle leaves

5 teaspoons (level) powdered gelatine

120 ml warm water

400 ml whipping cream

WILD LIME JELLY:

1 cup wild limes

200 g sugar

50 ml lime juice

500 ml apple juice

5 teaspoons (level) powdered gelatine

ORANGE SAUCE:

2 cups orange juice

1 tablespoon orange zest, julienned

100 g castor sugar

50 ml orange liqueur

2 tablespoons lime juice

2 teaspoons cornflour

Place the egg yolks and castor sugar in a stainless steel bowl and whisk until they are a pale creamy colour. Place the milk and the lemon myrtle leaves in a saucepan and heat until simmering. Pour half of the milk over the egg yolks stirring constantly, then add the remaining milk. Stir slowly over a low heat until the anglaise mixture is thick enough to coat the back of a spoon. Remove from heat and set the anglaise aside.

Dissolve the gelatine in the warm water. Stir the gelatine through the anglaise thoroughly. Allow to cool, but continue to stir occasionally. Remove and discard the lemon myrtle leaves. Place the whipping cream in a bowl and whip until soft peaks form. Gently fold the cream through the mixture, making sure it is well combined. Pour the mixture into a small dariole mould and refrigerate until set.

TO MAKE THE WILD LIME JELLY, place all the ingredients except the gelatine in a saucepan and bring to the boil. Stir in the gelatine until it has dissolved, then set aside to cool. Once the jelly is cool pour 1 cm of the jelly into the bottom of a large dariole mould and refrigerate until set.

When it is set turn out the small dariole mould and place the bavarois on the jelly in the large dariole mould. Pour jelly around the bavarois, filling the mould to the top with the remaining liquid jelly. Refrigerate until set.

TO MAKE THE ORANGE SAUCE, place the orange juice, zest, sugar, orange liquor and lime juice in a sauce pan and bring to the boil. Dilute the cornflour by mixing it with the lime juice. Mix the cornflour mixture through the orange sauce to thicken it. Allow to cool. To serve, turn out the bavoir and pour orange sauce over it.

ORANGE AND WATTLE SEED SORBET

500 ml water	2 tablespoons lemon juice
4 Bushells Orange and Wattle Seed teabags	1/2 tablespoon wattle seeds
80 g sugar	1 tablespoon Campari
1 1/2 cups freshly squeezed orange juice	1 egg white, beaten until stiff

Boil the water and infuse the teabags—the best results will be achieved if the teabags are infused overnight. Remove the bags and place the tea water into a saucepan with the sugar, orange juice, lemon juice and wattle seeds. Bring to the boil, remove from the heat and add the Campari. Cool and drain into an ice-cream machine (sorbets can only successfully be made in an ice-cream machine). When it is half-frozen, remove from the freezer and beat through the stiff egg white, then return to the freezer until completely frozen.

To serve, scoop the sorbet out with a spoon that has been run under hot water, and serve with fresh fruit or wafers or with pudding or other homemade icecream.

MACADAMIA NUT ICECREAM

10 egg yolks	1 vanilla bean, split
200 g castor sugar	200 g macadamia nuts, roughly chopped
1 litre cream	

Place the egg yolks and castor sugar in a stainless steel bowl and whisk until they are a pale creamy colour. Place the cream and the vanilla bean in a saucepan and heat until simmering. Remove the vanilla bean. Pour half the cream over the egg yolks stirring constantly, then add the remaining cream. Stir slowly over a low heat until the mixture is thick enough to coat the back of a spoon. Remove from heat and allow to cool. Add the macadamia nuts.

Pour the mixture into an icecream machine and churn until set. Freeze.

STRAWBERRY AND CRACKED PEPPERBERRY ICECREAM

10 egg yolks	2 punnets ripe strawberries, hulled
200 g castor sugar	2 tablespoons ground pepperberries
1 litre cream	1 nip strawberry liqueur
1 vanilla bean, split	

Place the egg yolks and castor sugar in a stainless steel bowl and whisk until they are a pale creamy colour. Place the cream and the vanilla bean in a saucepan and gently heat until simmering. Remove the vanilla bean. Pour half the cream over the egg yolks stirring constantly, then add the remaining cream. Stir slowly over a low heat until the mixture is thick enough to coat the back of a spoon. Remove from heat and allow to cool.

Purée the strawberries and mix into the anglaise. Strain to remove the seeds and the vanilla bean, then add the pepperberries and strawberry liquor.

Pour the mixture into an icecream machine and churn until set. Freeze until needed.

SAUCE
STOC
DRESS

GARLIC AND GINGER OIL

- 1 cup raw garlic, peeled and roughly chopped
- 1 cup green ginger, unpeeled and roughly chopped
- 3 cups vegetable oil

Purée all of the ingredients in a blender until very well combined. Use this oil as you would ordinary cooking oil, whenever the flavours of garlic and ginger will enhance the recipe.

This recipe makes 2 cups and will keep in a sealed jar in the refrigerator for up to 2 months.

WATERCRESS AND PEPPERLEAF OIL

- 1/2 bunch watercress
- 1 teaspoon pepperleaf
- 1 cup olive oil
- 1/2 teaspoon salt

Blanch the watercress in boiling water, remove and pat dry, then purée in a blender with the pepperleaf, olive oil and salt.

This recipe will keep in a sealed container in the refrigerator for 2 weeks.

LIGHT MAYONNAISE

- 2 egg yolks
- 1 teaspoon Dijon mustard
- 2 teaspoons white wine vinegar
- 1 cup good quality vegetable oil
- 4 teaspoons warm water

Whisk together the egg yolks, mustard and white wine vinegar in a bowl until light and fluffy. Continue whisking and add the oil, drop by drop. This can be time consuming, but the results are worth it—if you add the oil too quickly, the mixture will separate. The mixture should become creamy and thicken slowly; however, it will not be as thick as commercial mayonnaise. Stir the water gradually through the mixture.

This recipe makes 1 cup and will keep in a sealed jar in the refrigerator for up to 4 weeks.

LEMON MYRTLE DRESSING

3 tablespoons lemon myrtle	1 tablespoon Dijon mustard
100 ml water	50 ml white wine vinegar
3 egg yolks	500 ml vegetable oil

Combine the lemon myrtle and water in a saucepan. Bring to the boil over low heat (this brings out the flavour of the lemon myrtle), then remove from the heat and cool.

Vigorously whisk together the egg yolks, mustard and white wine vinegar until light and fluffy, then begin whisking in the oil a few drops at a time until the dressing is the consistency of thick cream. Whisk in the lemon myrtle and water.

This recipe makes 1 litre or 4 cups and will keep in a sealed jar in the refrigerator for up to 4 weeks.

LEMON ASPEN MAYONNAISE

11/2 egg yolks	1 small pinch saffron threads
1 tablespoon dijon mustard	1 teaspoon warm water
21/2 teaspoons white wine vinegar	60 ml lemon aspen juice
1 cup vegetable oil	salt and pepper, to taste

Vigorously whisk together the egg yolks, mustard and white wine vinegar until light and fluffy, then begin whisking in the oil a few drops at a time until the dressing is the consistency of thick cream.

Dissolve the saffron threads in the water, then add to the dressing with the lemon aspen juice and mustard. Combine thoroughly and season with the salt and pepper, then add water to desired consistency.

This recipe makes 3 cups and will keep in a sealed jar in the refrigerator for up to 3 weeks.

BLACK BEAN DRESSING

3 tablespoons black beans
   or black bean paste
1/4 bunch chervil
1 x 2.5 cm knob ginger

2 cloves garlic
250 ml vegetable oil
1 tablespoon ketchip manis
1 tablespoon Yuensan

Purée all of the ingredients well in a blender.
   This recipe makes 1 cup and will keep in a sealed jar in the refrigerator for up to 2 weeks.

OVEN-DRIED ROMANO TOMATOES

romano tomatoes
good quality olive oil

sea salt and freshly ground black pepper, to taste
fresh or dried herbs e.g. basil, parsley, sage, rosemary, optional

Slice the tomatoes in halves or quarters, depending on the size you want them.
Arrange on a baking tray with rack, then brush generously with virgin olive oil.
Sprinkle the tomatoes with the sea salt, pepper and herbs. Bake at 120°C for several
hours, basting with the olive oil every hour, until they start to dry out and are not too
withered, still holding their shape. How well dried the tomatoes are is a question of
personal taste. Experiment a little, moister tomatoes are good for some dishes, while
drier ones are better for others.
   The tomatoes will keep in a covered container in the refrigerator for several days.

ILLAWARRA PLUM SALSA

500 g Illawarra plums, halved

200 ml balsamic vinegar

100 ml honey

20 ml fish sauce

1 red chilli, de-seeded and finely chopped

1 bay leaf

200 ml red wine

juice and zest of 1 orange

juice and zest of 1 lemon

1/2 bunch basil

1 clove garlic, finely chopped

1/2 Spanish onion

10 pink peppercorns

Place the plums, vinegar, honey, fish sauce, chilli, bay leaf and red wine in a stainless steel saucepan. Bring to the boil, reduce the heat and simmer for 15 minutes. Remove from the heat and cool.

When cool, add the remaining ingredients.

This recipe makes 500 g and will keep in a sealed jar in the refrigerator for up to 2 weeks.

PANDANA LEAF SAUCE

1/2 cup malt vinegar

4 tablespoons ginger, finely chopped

4 cups water

1/2 cup soy sauce

1/2 cup brown sugar

1 medium brown onion, peeled and quartered

1 pandana leaf, julienned

1 teaspoon arrowroot or cornflour, optional

Combine all of the ingredients except the arrowroot in a saucepan and simmer steadily until reduced by one-third and the mixture coats the back of a spoon. Strain through a fine sieve. If necessary, place a small quantity of sauce into a cup, combine with the arrowroot and return to the sauce in the pan, stirring constantly until the sauce thickens.

This recipe makes 4 cups and can be stored in a sealed jar in the refrigerator for 2 months. The sauce is also a delicious accompaniment to stir-fried and seafood dishes.

BUSH TOMATO SAUCE

3 tablespoons bush tomato

2 small red chillies, de-seeded and chopped

2 tablespoons oil

12 medium tomatoes, roughly chopped

1 teaspoon brown sugar

1 teaspoon balsamic vinegar

1 sheet compressed dried seaweed

2 cups water

1 cup white wine

salt and pepper, to taste

Fry the bush tomato and chillies in the oil until the bush tomato browns, then add the next 4 ingredients. Simmer for 10 minutes, then add the water and white wine. Cook until the tomatoes are tender, remove from the heat and purée. Serve hot.

This recipe makes 3 cups and will keep in a sealed container in the refrigerator for 2 weeks.

CHEESEFRUIT SAUCE

1/2 pineapple, roughly chopped

250 g Tallegio cheese, roughly chopped

100 g blue cheese, roughly chopped

3 cloves garlic, chopped

2 cups cream

2 tablespoons turmeric

Place all of the ingredients in a saucepan and simmer uncovered for 20 minutes. Remove from the heat, purée in a blender and strain.

This recipe makes 2 cups of sauce and will keep in a covered container in the refrigerator for 1 week.

SEAFOOD AND PALMASAMI PARCELS WITH BUSH TOMATO SAUCE PAGE **62**

CARAMEL SAUCE

300 g brown sugar	300 ml thickened cream
60 ml white wine	juice of 1 lime
125 g butter	

To make the caramel sauce, place the brown sugar and the white wine in a thick-bottomed saucepan and bring to the boil. Simmer until the sugar starts to dissolve and turns into a caramel consistency. Take off the heat and add butter, cream and lime juice. Put back on a low heat and stir until all ingredients are well combined. Set aside to cool, ready for use hot or cold.

This recipe will keep in a sealed jar in the refrigerator for up to 4 weeks.

PALMASAMI

200 g warrigal greens or spinach	150 g solid block pure coconut cream, grated
2 medium brown onions, finely chopped	salt and pepper, to taste

Combine all of the ingredients and wrap tightly in aluminium foil to make a watertight parcel. Place the parcel in a baking dish or saucepan of water. Poach in the oven at 180°C or on the stovetop in a saucepan for about 30 minutes or until the warrigal greens and onions are tender. Remove from the water, unwrap the parcel and purée the contents into a paste. Cool.

RED BALL CHILLIES STUFFED WITH EMU PAGE 63

BASIC LEMON MYRTLE AND LIME CURRY SAUCE

4 tablespoons Garlic and Ginger Oil	1 tablespoon ground coriander
(see recipe page 158)	1 teaspoon turmeric
1 tablespoon red curry paste	400 ml cream
1/2 cup Palmasami (see recipe page 165)	400 ml coconut cream
juice and zest of 2 lemons	4 lemon myrtle leaves or 1 tablespoon ground lemon myrtle
1 tablespoon ground cumin	

Fry the curry paste in the Garlic and Ginger Oil, stirring briskly, for 2–3 minutes or until aromatic. Add the remaining ingredients, combine well, and simmer for 10 minutes or until the sauce is thick enough to coat the back of a spoon.

WARRIGAL GREEN AND MACADAMIA NUT PESTO

1/2 cup macadamia nuts,	2 cups chopped warrigal greens
roasted in the oven	1/2 bunch chopped fresh basil
1/2 cup grated parmesan cheese	salt and pepper, to taste
1 1/2 cups olive oil	

Puree the macadamia nuts, parmesan and 1/4 cup of the olive oil in a blender. Add the remaining ingredients and the remaining oil and purée until smooth.

This recipe makes 2 cups and will keep in a covered container in the refrigerator for 4 weeks.

LEMON MYRTLE HOLLANDAISE

300 g butter

4 egg yolks

juice of 2 lemons

2 tablespoons lemon myrtle

Clarify the butter by melting it in a small saucepan over low heat until it separates into two distinct parts, a cloudy liquid (ghee) which falls to the bottom of the pan, and clear (clarified) butter at the top.

Place the egg yolks, lemon juice and lemon myrtle into either a stainless steel bowl set over a large pot of boiling water, a double boiler, or a small saucepan that will sit nicely over a larger saucepan of boiling water and whisk over the heated water until the yolks become light and fluffy and stick to the whisk in stretchy 'ribbons' when drawn away from the mixture. Gradually add the clarified butter to the egg yolk mixture, drop by drop and whisking constantly, until only the ghee remains. Discard the ghee. The hollandaise is ready when it is the consistency of runny mayonnaise.

NATIVE MINT PESTO

1/2 cup pine nuts

1 cup olive oil

1/2 cup grated parmesan cheese

1 1/2 tablespoon native mint

1/2 bunch basil, stems removed, roughly chopped

1/2 bunch mint, stems removed, roughly chopped

salt and pepper, to taste

Lightly roast the pine nuts on a baking tray at 150°C for 5 minutes or until golden. Purée the nuts with a quarter of the oil, then add the parmesan cheese, mint, basil, native mint, salt and pepper and the remaining oil. Purée well.

Serve the pesto with fish, lamb or pasta, or add to dressings for a fresh twist.

This recipe makes 2 cups and will keep in a sealed jar in the refrigerator for up to 2 weeks.

LIGHT BATTER

2 1/2 cups plain flour	1 egg
5 teaspoons baking powder	500 ml beer or water
salt and pepper	

Sift together all the dry ingredients. Make a well in the middle and slowly whisk in the egg and then the beer or water. Whisk thoroughly to ensure there are no lumps. Refrigerate until needed.

VEGETABLE STOCK

1 kg carrots, roughly chopped	2 bay leaves
1 kg onions, roughly chopped	1 sprig thyme
4 sticks celery, roughly chopped	6 peppercorns, crushed
4 leeks, roughly chopped	5 litres water
1 whole bulb garlic, roughly chopped	

Combine all of the ingredients in a large stock pot and cook, simmering, for 3–4 hours. Remove from the heat and strain.

This recipe makes 4.5 litres and will keep in a sealed container in the refrigerator for up to 7–10 days or in the freezer for 6 months.

FISH STOCK

5 kg fish bones (your fishmonger will be
   able to supply these)
1 celery stick, roughly chopped
3 carrots, roughly chopped

2 onions, roughly chopped
1 leek, roughly chopped
6 litres water

Combine all of the ingredients in a large stock pot, bring to the boil, reduce the heat and cook, simmering, for 25 minutes. Remove from the heat and strain.

   This recipe makes 5.5 litres and will keep in a sealed container in the refrigerator for up to 3–4 days or for 3 months in the freezer.

BEEF STOCK

2 kg beef bone
1/2 kg veal shank
300 g pork trotters
1 carrot, roughly chopped
1 celery stick, roughly chopped
1 leek, roughly chopped
1 onion, roughly chopped
2 bay leaves

5 peppercorns
1 sprig thyme
1 whole knob garlic, halved
500 ml red wine
3 litres water
200 ml red wine vinegar
2 tablespoons tomato paste

Arrange the bones in a flame-proof baking dish and bake at 180°C for about 1 hour or until they are well browned. Remove the bones to a large stock pot.

   Set the baking dish on the stovetop and fry the remaining non-liquid ingredients in the pan juice and fat until they are well softened. Add these ingredients to the stock pot with the red wine, water, red wine vinegar and tomato paste. Cook at a bare simmer for 5–6 hours, adding water from time to time if necessary to make sure the water level remains above the bones at all times, and skimming off any scum that rises to the top with a large spoon or similar.

   When the stock is well flavoured, strain, discard the bones and vegetables and refrigerate. When cold, remove any fat that solidifies on the surface.

   This recipe makes 2–3 litres of stock (depending on how often you top up the water level) and will keep in a sealed container in the refrigerator for up to 1 week or for 3–4 months in the freezer.

CHICKEN STOCK

5 kg chicken bones (your local poultry store or butcher can supply these)	1 leek, roughly chopped
2 carrots, roughly chopped	2 bay leaves
1 stick celery, roughly chopped	5 peppercorns
1 onion, roughly chopped	1 sprig thyme
6 cloves garlic, roughly chopped	3 litres water

Combine all of the ingredients in a large stock pot or similar, bring to the boil, reduce the heat and cook at a bare simmer for 3 hours, skimming off any scum that rises to the top with a large spoon.

When the stock is well flavoured, strain, discard the bones and vegetables and refrigerate. When cold, remove any fat that solidifies on the surface.

This recipe makes 5 litres and will keep in a sealed container in the refrigerator for up to 1 week or in the freezer for 3–4 months.

KANGAROO STOCK

2 1/2 kg kangaroo bones (your supplier will be able to give you these)	6 cloves garlic, roughly chopped
500 g pig's trotters	1 sprig thyme
1 carrot, roughly chopped	5 peppercorns
1 stick celery, roughly chopped	2 bay leaves
1 onion, roughly chopped	300 ml red wine
1 leek, roughly chopped	3 litres water

Arrange the bones and vegetables on a couple of baking trays—don't worry if you have to pack them tightly—and bake at 180°C for about 1 hour or until the bones are well browned and the vegetables are soft.

Combine the baked ingredients with the garlic, thyme, peppercorns, bay leaves, red wine and water in a large pot. Cook at a bare simmer for 8–12 hours or until the stock is well flavoured. Remove from the heat, strain and discard the bones and vegetables. Refrigerate and remove any fat that solidifies on the surface.

This recipe makes 3-4 litres and will keep in a sealed container in the refrigerator for up to 1 week or in the freezer for 3–4 months.

JUS RECIPES

Throughout the book, you will have noticed that many recipes call for the addition of a jus, or a sauce based on a jus, which is a sauce made from stock. All types of stock can be reduced to form a sauce, however, beef or kangaroo stock when reduced will become thicker than chicken or fish stock because of their relatively high gelatine content (gelatine being a protein derived from bones.) Wine should always be added to stock both for its flavour and colour-enhancing properties.

The following are some basic recipes for sauces derived from beef and kangaroo stocks. It is important, especially with darker-coloured stocks such as these, that they are reduced slowly, to ensure optimum colour and flavour. Once the reduction is complete the stock becomes a jus to which various different flavour elements can be introduced.

KANGAROO JUS

2 tablespoons redcurrant jelly	8–10 sprigs lemon thyme
500 ml red wine	6 litres kangaroo stock
1 onion, sliced finely	salt and pepper, to taste
1/4 bulb garlic	

Cook the redcurrant jelly and red wine in a saucepan over low heat until the liquid has reduced by half. Add the next four ingredients to the reduced liquid, bring to the boil and barely simmer for 2–3 hours or until the liquid is the consistency of light syrup and coats the back of a spoon lightly. Season to taste and strain.

This recipe makes 1 cup of jus and will keep in the refrigerator for up to 6–8 days or in the freezer for 3–4 months.

PEPPERBERRY JUS BASED ON KANGAROO STOCK

2 tablespoons redcurrant jelly	8–10 sprigs lemon thyme
500 ml red wine	6 litres kangaroo stock
1 onion, sliced finely	8 pepperberries, ground
1/4 bulb garlic	salt and pepper, to taste

Cook the redcurrant jelly and red wine in a saucepan over low heat until the liquid has reduced by half. Add the next four ingredients to the reduced liquid, bring to the boil and barely simmer for 2–3 hours or until the liquid is the consistency of light syrup and coats the back of a spoon lightly. Add the pepperberries in the last half hour of cooking. Season to taste and strain.

This recipe makes 1 cup of jus and will keep in the refrigerator for up to 6–8 days or in the freezer for 3–4 months.

BEEF JUS

1 tablespoon redcurrant jelly

500 ml red wine

1 onion

1/4 bulb garlic

3-4 sprigs lemon thyme

2 litres beef stock

salt and pepper, to taste

Combine the redcurrant jelly and red wine in a saucepan over low heat until the liquid has reduced by half. Add the remaining ingredients to the reduced liquid, bring to the boil and barely simmer for 2–3 hours or until the liquid is the consistency of light syrup and coats the back of a spoon lightly. Season to taste and strain.

This recipe makes 1 cup of jus and will keep in the refrigerator for up to 7–10 days or in the freezer for 3 months.

CHICKEN AND WILD LIME JUS

500 ml white wine

2 litres chicken stock

15 wild limes, roughly chopped

2 cloves garlic, finely chopped

1 chilli, de-seeded and finely chopped

1/2 tablespoon cumin

1/2 bunch dill, finely chopped

salt and pepper, to taste

1 teaspoon cornflour, optional

Combine the wine, stock and wild limes in a saucepan over low heat until the liquid has reduced to 1 litre. Add the garlic, chilli, cumin, dill and salt and pepper.

To thicken the sauce if necessary or desired, remove 1 tablespoon or so of the jus to a cup, mix in the cornflour to form a loose paste, then stir this mixture through the jus over low heat until the cornflour begins to do its work.

This recipe makes 2 cups and will keep in a covered container in the refrigerator for up to 1 week.

GLOSSARY

Bush Tomato (Akudjura)

Akudjura is one Aboriginal name for the native bush tomato which is a strong flavoured fruit from the desert, tasting of tamarillo and caramel.

It is easy to use in its ground form. Use as a condiment and also in sauces, stuffings and soups. Sauté with butter or margarine to enhance the flavour.

Bunya Nuts

These nuts are similar in size and flavour to chestnuts and were a feasting food of Aborigines in the Bunya Mountains of southern Queensland.

Bunya nuts are shaped like an overgrown almond, with a shell similar to a coconut husk. To eat, tear the nuts out of the husks. Each nut is encased in a thin woody shell. Boil for approximately one hour until the shells split. Halve them with a knife and remove from shells.

Suitable for any dish, with fruit ingredients in particular, similar to chestnut.

SUBSTITUTE: chestnut dried or fresh.

Bush Cucumbers

These globular shaped cucumbers are tiny and fresh green in colour with a slight speckle or faint stripe marking their skins. The skin is quite bitter, but the ripe flesh inside is sweet and has a refreshing flavour of cucumber with distinct mint overtones. The Aboriginal people of the arid outback regions have long valued the bush cucumber as a food plant.

Similar to telegraph and apple cucumber in flavour but very juicy, hard skinned with a delicate flesh, varying in size from an olive to a small roman tomato.

Can be used in salads, pickled and served warm or cold in starters and main courses.

If the skin is tough, blanch for 15 minutes in pickling liquid.

SUBSTITUTE: telegraph or apple cucumber.

Cheesefruit

Cheesefruit combines a pineapple flavour with a blue vein cheese taste which sounds unusual but is actually delicious.

It is available usually in liquid form, but if bought fresh the juice can be extracted. Ideal for starters and mains, suitable with polenta timbales and sauces. It has a very strong flavour.

SUBSTITUTE: A purée of light blue cheese and pineapple.

Davidson Plums

These are large crimson rainforest fruits, from a deep red coloured bush.

Fleshy and tart-flavoured, they are ideal when poached or stewed. They can also be puréed in sauces and dressings. The whole fruit is a good companion for desserts — e.g. icecream, sorbets, soufflés or can be used in pies, tarts, cakes and puddings.

Davidson plums also marry well as a sauce with game and poultry and work well blended with chilli. The plum has a big robust flavour.

Desert Lime

See Tropical Wild Lime.

Illawarra Plum

This fruit from the south coast of NSW is plum-like in flavour with a pleasant yet subtle resinous quality. Seedless and the same size as other plums, the Illawarra plum can be sauced and performs extremely well with chilli or ginger.

Illawarra plums are best used cooked in starters and main courses or as a magnificent, flavoursome salsa, ideal with octopus, game and red meats. In a sauce they lose some of their unique flavour (which is why a salsa is more interesting). They're good in desserts — e.g. icecream, puddings, pies and tarts.

SUBSTITUTE: Green plum and cassis liqueur.

Kakadu Plum

The kakadu plum is an olive-sized fruit with a mild apricot flavour, which has been found to be the world's highest fruit source of vitamin C.

Like an olive to look at, the flesh holds onto the seed but can be simply cut away. The kakadu plum is at its best when used in stuffings or as a paste, tapenade, purée or pickle.

SUBSTITUTE: Raw green olives — though almost inedible when raw its character is changed in the cooking process.

Lemon Aspen

This tangy yellow citrus-flavoured fruit comes from an east coast rainforest tree and is as versatile as the lemon.

It takes on diverse flavours and tastes according to whether the juice or the fresh fruit is used, which makes it a very interesting ingredient. When using the fruit, remove the hard core and use the flesh for marinades, sauces and salsas. It can also be used in cocktails — e.g. aspen daquiris and margaritas. Try it also in desserts such as icecreams and tarts.

Lemon aspens are available as fruit or juice.
SUBSTITUTE: fresh grapefruit or lime juice.

Lemon Myrtle

From a rainforest tree on the east coast of Australia, the lemon myrtle leaf when crushed or infused releases a tempting combination of taste and aroma similar to a blend of sweet lemon grass, lemon and lime oils.

Lemon myrtle is wonderful in starters, mains and desserts but must not be overcooked. Use whole fresh leaves if available and dried if not. If using dried leaves, sprinkle into the dish at the end of cooking. Dried lemon myrtle is ideal in sauces, as a coating when grilling or baking and in icecreams, sorbets and creme brulée.

Lemon myrtle is suitable in any recipe that includes lime leaves or lemon grass. In Asian food, it can be used instead of lemon grass.
SUBSTITUTE: lemon grass, lime leaves.

Macadamia nuts

Macadamia nuts are Australia's first commercially-grown native species. Try roasting them to accent their flavour. Well blended they make a great nut butter or thickening agent; chopped, use them as a topping on cakes and other desserts. The nuts are high in fat but cholesterol-free.
SUBSTITUTE: almonds.

Munthari Berries

Commonly called native cranberries, munthari are small green and red fruits with the flavour of Granny Smith apples.

Munthari are one of the most versatile of all our fruits, used whole in sauces for starters, mains, salsas and desserts.

Like a tart Granny Smith apple or nashi pear with a light cinnamon flavour, munthari are beautiful with poultry, game, seafood and all types of desserts.

Native Aniseed

Native aniseed comes in whole form. It can be used in sauces, dressings, stuffings and coatings. It is an extremely delicate and subtle aniseed, excellent blended in salads. It also makes beautiful icecream, with a much cleaner flavour than liquorice.
SUBSTITUTE: dried fennel, five star anise or fresh fennel for salads.

Native Mint, Native Peppermint

The native mint bush has very small rounded leaves that smell and taste distinctly of mint, even though this plant is not a true mint. While the flavour of the leaf is decidedly minty, it has a secondary peppery taste that is aromatic and very pleasing.
SUBSTITUTE: mint.

Native Thyme

Available dried and ground, this is light green with a flavour similar to a combination of tarragon, thyme and rosemary. Use it to flavour dishes as a dried herb and a condiment.
SUBSTITUTE: mixed dried herbs.

Pandana Leaf

Pandanus leaves come from a distinctive small tree. Up to 1 metre long, the leaves are arranged in spirals and crowd on the ends of branches. Pandanus occurs on exposed coastal headlands and along beaches north from Port Macquarie to Queensland.

Paperbark

Paperbark grows with scented leaves and papery bark. Hold a leaf up to the light and see its shiny oil glands, then crush it to smell the aromatic oils. It is common in coastal swamps and around lake margins.

This is the Aboriginal answer to aluminium foil, banana leaves for a clay pot and lotus leaves.

Paperbark needs to be submerged in water for 10–15 minutes to make it pliable. Fish, meat, poultry and rice can all be wrapped in paperbark and barbecued, baked or poached. Food cooked in paperbark sometimes develops a light smoky flavour.
SUBSTITUTE: aluminium foil.

Pepperberry

These small purple/black berries have a hot peppery zing and can flavour or garnish almost any sauce or can be baked into a unique pepperbread.

Pepperberries contain a definite unique flavour — aromatic, big and bold. They are very hot. Use them them in starters, mains and desserts. In savoury sauces they can be used for game, poultry (used sparingly), red meats, emu, kangaroo and magpie goose. They are wonderful in icecream (e.g. strawberry and pepperberry) and are ideal with most fruits, berries in particular.

When crushed or ground in a mortar and pestle, the flavour disperses rapidly through the other ingredients.
SUBSTITUTE: black peppercorns.

Pepperleaf

The alpine mountain pepperleaf can be used dry or ground and added to hot dishes as a seasoning or used whole like bay leaves. It has a smooth woody character with a hot zing somewhere between pepper and chilli which reduces with cooking.

With their fresh peppery flavour, pepperleaves are a perfect substitute for white pepper. They can be infused in sauces, casseroles, ragouts, timbales and brulées and used on the kitchen or restaurant table as we do at Edna's.
SUBSTITUTE: pepper.

Quandongs

Sometimes called wild or desert peaches, these red fruits have a tart apricot and peach flavour. The kernels of the fruit are also highly flavoured.

Quandongs are excellent in sweet and sour dishes, salsas, sauces, dressings, pies, puddings, chutneys and jams. Delicate yet tart in flavour, they go well with chilli and are well suited to use in Asian stir fries.

The quandong kernel needs to be dried then pan fried in oil till dark (almost burnt) and ground by hand. It has a light, nutty sesame flavour, ideal for Asian-style sauces, but it must be strained before being added to the main ingredients.
SUBSTITUTE: unripe peach using skin and a small amount of flesh.

Rosella Buds

The tropical rosella buds of the wild hibiscus have a crispy berry and rhubarb taste. They are famous for the jams and chutneys they flavour so well and lend themselves to use in pie fillings and other pastries, icecreams, sorbets and fruit stews.

Samphire

Samphire is an interesting-looking plant, often referred to as sea fennel. Its smooth-skinned stem is segmented along its length and varies in colour from a deep olive green to a deep red, changing with the seasons. The flavour of the stem is salty, like snake beans.

It must firstly be blanched, and can then be used in stir fried Asian salads, pickled and used as a garnish or as a base for starters and main courses.

Tropical Wild Lime

Sourced from several native Australian citrus species, these fruits can be found from rainforests to arid areas. They have a very strong, tart lime flavour and an edible though slightly bitter yellow/green skin.

Tropical wild limes have a unique flavour and are more versatile than the other variety of native limes, the desert lime. They can be used in sauces, stuffings, salsa, dressings and desserts — e.g. brulées, coulis, icecreams, sorbets and (mixed with other fruits) tarts.

They usually need blanching because of their sharpness but remember the flavour is exciting and distinctive.

Desert limes are much larger and stranger than tropical wild limes. They are best used — carefully — in sauces or in chutney and relish or pickled. They can be ideal in jam as their flavour becomes more intense when sweetened. The desert lime tastes very different to the tropical wild lime.
SUBSTITUTE: fresh lime or Chinese preserved lime.

Warrigal Greens

This is the native equivalent to English spinach. Captain Cook dined on warrigal greens and stingray in 1770. Long before this the Aborigines in the inland were eating the new tips off the same species.

Warrigal greens is another very versatile vegetable, ideal for stir fries, stuffing timbales and salads. Unlike English spinach it has its own in-built, sturdy personality.
SUBSTITUTE: English spinach.

Wattleseed

These are the seeds of a particular dryland wattle which are roasted and ground to produce a coffee-chocolate-hazelnut flavour.

Wattleseed is usually used in desserts, where it excels. It has a light mocca flavour which goes well in icecream, brulèe, creme anglaise, bavarois and mousse, and blended with white or dark chocolate.

It can also be used in savoury dishes such as blinis, sauces and coatings — however it needs to be roasted to develop its flavour. It comes in ground form and can be used as a non-caffeine substitute, Wattlecino, in an espresso machine.
SUBSTITUTE: ground hazelnuts.

FIRST CATCH YOUR SUPPER — THE SUPPLIERS

It's not nearly so hard to find supplies of native Australian ingredients as it was ten years ago. There's a small band of wholesalers able to ship produce around Australia and overseas, and some of our more enterprising supermarkets, delis and butchers have begun to stock certain lines. The ones we know about are listed here, but the pattern is always changing and if there's no outlet near you it's worth asking in local shops. A good butcher will have no difficulty in getting hold of kangaroo meat for you, and delis can easily order the herbs and oils.

The important thing to remember is that these ingredients are what the land naturally produces. You may find that the tree on the corner with the little bluish fruits you've been squashing underfoot for years is in fact an Illawarra plum. If you keep pots of herbs on the windowsill, as we did in the flat in Pyrmont all those years ago, it's easy enough to try out some cuttings of lemon myrtle or native mint, and if you're lucky enough to have a vegetable garden you could plant bush tomato seeds or warrigal greens. It's our dream that every household in Australia will one day have these wonderful flavours as part of their daily diet, as essential as parsley and potatoes.

The following businesses not only supply the goods but in most cases will help with information if you live outside their delivery area.

Australia wide

BUSH TUCKER SUPPLY COMPANY
482 Victoria Rd, Gladesville 2111
Tel: 02 9817 1060, toll free (from outside 02 area): 1800 696 496
Fax: 02 9817 3587
Website: www.bushtucker.com.au
Extensive selection of all native products. Vik Cherikoff will supply information for all areas, and the website gives contact numbers for all States and Territories

FRANKLINS BIG FRESH
SELECTED COLES STORES
These supermarkets carry a selection of dried herbs, oils and other products

New South Wales

NATIONAL MEAT SUPPLIES
9 Sloane St, Marrickville 2204
Tel: 02 9557 5760
Fax: 02 9519 8378
Specialist in kangaroo, emu and crocodile. Alan East will supply information

SOUTHERN GAME MEATS
22 Churchill St, North Auburn 2165
Tel: 02 9748 2261
Kangaroo wholesaler

CHIPPY'S FOOD DISTRIBUTORS
2 Lilian Fowler Place, Marrickville 2204
Tel: 02 9550 4022
Wholesaler of fresh, dried and frozen native fruit, vegetables and herbs

ESSENTIAL INGREDIENTS
6 Australia St, Camperdown 2050
Tel: 02 9550 5477
Wholesaler and retailer of an extensive selection of produce

DOWNTON & DYER
7 Wollongong Rd, Arncliffe 2205
Tel: 02 9599 1344
Fax: 02 9597 5763
Wholesaler also supplying Canberra, Wollongong, Orange and Newcastle

ALL STATES FOOD SERVICES
Warehouse M, Flemington Markets, Flemington 2129
Tel: 02 9746 6342
Fax: 02 9746 6342
Fruit and vegetable merchants stocking a selection of native produce

DAVID JONES FOOD HALL
Corner Market and Castlereagh Sts, Sydney 2000
Tel: 02 9266 5544
Retailer

BLACKWATTLE DELI
Sydney Fish Markets, Pyrmont 2009
Tel: 02 9552 3591
Retailer

FIVE STAR GOURMET DELI
13 Willoughby Rd, Crows Nest 2065
Tel: 02 9438 5666
Fax: 02 9966 0269
Retailer

BORONIA BAKERY
95 Pittwater Rd, Hunters Hill 2110
Tel: 02 9817 1162
Specialist in native flavoured breads

IDEAS ON FOOD
8/13 Parson St, Rozelle 2039
Tel: 02 9555 9688
Fax: 02 9555 9388

BUSHFOODS OF AUSTRALIA/NATIVE
TASTES
Dudgeons Lane, Bangalow 2479
Tel: 02 6687 1005
Fax: 02 6687 1358
Wholesalers of a wide selection of herbs,
oils, preserves and other products

MIRABOOK
Myrtle Mountain Road, Candelo 2550
Tel: 06 493 2327

INTEGRITY FOODS, CENTRAL COAST
PO Box 4236, Lakehaven 2263
Tel: 02 4392 4496
Fax: 02 4392 4381

COFFS PROVIDORES
Coffs Harbour 2450
Tel: 02 6685 2888
Fax: 02 6658 2833

Victoria
THE VITAL INGREDIENT
206 Clarendon St, South Melbourne 3205
Tel: 03 9696 3511
Retailer

ROBINS BUSH FOODS
39 Lothian St, North Melbourne 3051
Tel: 03 9326 6188
Wholesaler only. Run by Julie Robins,
author of *Wild Limes*

DAIMARU FOOD HALL
211 La Trobe St, Melbourne 3000
Tel: 03 9160 6666
Retailer

CAMERON AND PHILIPPE
Stall 82-84, Shed 1, Queen Victoria
Markets, cnr Elizabeth and Victoria Sts,
Melbourne 3000
Tel: 03 9329 3909
Retailers

ROSEBUDS
233 Williamsons Rd, Templestowe 3106
Tel: 03 9846 4591

Queensland
JOLIFFE'S OUTBACK
3/14b Tennyson Memorial St, Yeerongpilly
4105
Tel: 07 3217 1999
Fax: 07 3217 1555
Wholesaler and distributor

BURLEIGH MARR
347 Lytton Rd, Morningside 4170
Tel: 07 3999 1999
Fax: 07 3217 1555
Seafood and general produce distributor

AUSTRALIAN TROPICAL AND NATIVE
FOODS
4 Bradford St, Whitfield, Cairns 4870
Tel: 070 537 458
Mobile: 019 484 422
Wholesaler and retailer

South Australia
AUSTRALIAN NATIVE PRODUCE
Production Kitchen:
87 Harrison Rd, Dudley Park 5008
Tel: 08 8346 3337
Fax: 03 8346 3387
Nursery & Farm:
Box 163, Paringa 5340
Tel/fax: 08 8595 1611
Wholesaler, supplier of seeds and plants
and developer of Red Ochre brand
products

THE TALL AUSTRALIAN
233 South Rd, Mile End 5031
Tel: 08 8354 2288
Fax: 08 8354 2038
Specialist in emu products

FIENA FOODS
77-79 Orsmond St, Hindmarsh 5008
Tel: 08 8346 9131

Tasmania
TASMANIAN GOURMET DISTRIBUTORS
Westbury Rd, Launceston
Tel: 03 6344 2902
Mobile: 018 139 707
Perth: 03 6398 2289
Wholesaler and retailer. Will assist with
information

LENAH GAME MEATS
George Town Rd, Rocherlea 7248
Tel: 03 6326 7696
Wholesaler of native meats

FOUR WAYS SUPERMARKET
Four Ways, Devonport 7310
Tel: 03 6424 5361

WURSTHAUS KITCHEN
Montpelier St, Salamander, Hobart 7000
Tel: 03 6224 0644

SEVEN DAY SUPERSTORE
Elizabeth St, North Hobart 7000
Retailer

Western Australia
THE GROCER
145 Stirling Hwy, Nedland 6009
Fax: 08 9389 8194

Northern Territory
PARAP FINE FOODS
40 Parap Rd, Parap, Darwin 0820
Tel: 08 8981 8597

INDEX